Lipstick and Legacies

Holly Byrd Miller
Visionary Author

Co-Authored By:
Tanya Battle, Julie Hill, Reba Hollingsworth,
Catina Jones, Grace Washington

Edited, Formatted and Published by Empower Her Publishing, LLC

TABLE OF CONTENTS

FOREWORD

Lipstick and Legacies is a wonderful collection of "her-stories" from six distinguished women who share their lives with us. They discuss their backgrounds, journeys to their present successes, and the hurdles that they encountered along those journeys. They have dedicated their lives to making their dreams come true no matter what life throws at them. We can all be inspired by these stories and use them as fuel to ignite or reinvigorate our own journeys. What a wonderful gift they have given us! Learn from them as you traverse the roads that lead to the fulfillment of your dreams; find the joy of self-expression and smart business habits; BELIEVE, and then pass it on.

As Reba Hollingsworth states in the book:

"Knowledge is power. What I know about starting and operating a business helps no one if I keep it a secret. That knowledge has the power to trickle down to other new business owners. Secondly, I can offer my support. I can financially support small businesses as a customer. I can also support with a simple email, card, or text that says "I see you. Keep up the great work!" I can't stress this enough: we need each other."

Daphne Maxwell Reid
Entrepreneur

DAPHNE MAXWELL REID

Daphne Maxwell Reid is best known as Aunt Vivian from the hit comedy, *The Fresh Prince of Bel-Air*. Her 40-year acting career is still vital with roles on many new television programs including starring and guest-starring roles on TV and in film: *Jacqueline & Jilly, Harriet, The Business of Christmas I & II, Trophy Wife, Bel-Air,* and *Fantasy Island*.

Her involvement in the community at-large rounds out a full schedule while presently serving on the Richmond Ballet Board and ChildFund International Board.

Daphne Maxwell Reid is an avid photographer of DOORS from around the world and is exhibiting and selling her collection entitled "Daphne Maxwell Reid's Fresh Prints®" at speaking engagements, art gatherings and on her website: www.DaphneMaxwellReid.com.

Four beautifully published books of her photographs, *DOORS, Opening Closed Doors: Cuba 2015, Belgium: Doors Old & New*, and *France*, accounts of her worldwide journeys to capture the portals, are available on her website. Also available on the website is *Grace, Soul & Motherwit: A Cookbook Spiced with Personal Memories*. She has taken her international door photos and created a fabric from which she makes a limited edition of her beautifully lined tote bags. Daphne collaborated with Stacy Hawkins Adams, a Richmond author of wonderful books, to create a note card collection of Daphne's photos and Stacy's thoughtful messages.

In keeping with her desire to express all facets of her creativity, Daphne has launched her custom made, wearable art collection: Chinese silk brocade "toppers" called Daphne Style. She has also created a collection of face masks with removable HEPA filters. Yes, she custom makes them all herself.

You Can Do More

Tanya Battle

It was the summer of 1971 in Harlem, New York. Afros were popular, bell-bottom pants were in, and mini-skirts, bright colors and patterns were everything. R&B music permeated the airways day and night. Marvin Gaye's "What's Going On?," Aretha Franklin's "Spanish Harlem," The Jackson 5's "Never Can Say Goodbye," and James Brown's "Make it Funky" were playing on constant rotation. Block parties, cook-outs, and dances were what everyone looked forward to. This is also the time when I came into the world.

On August 3, 1971, my beautiful 19-year-old mother who had long black hair, a slim build with nice legs gave birth to me. From what I have been told, I was born with a sweet smile and a calm demeanor. My grandmother said I never cried for anything. She and my mother would take turns checking on me because they never knew if I needed to be changed or fed. This is funny to me because I am still like that to this day. If something is bothering me, one would never know it. My dad was there to help, but it was the ladies in the house who made sure I was taken care of.

Reading about New York in the 1970s one learns about all of the crime and problems that seemed to plague the city. However, I don't have those kinds of memories at all. We had a very close-knit family that gathered often and shared many good times. My parents moved to the Bronx when I was about nine or ten months old. By the time I was fourteen months my parents welcomed my little brother into the family. I also had an older sister by my dad who spent time with us. Within a couple of years we moved to White Plains, NY. This was a "moving on up" moment like the popular television show of the 1970s, *The Jeffersons*. My dad and his business partners owned several restaurants and lounges in Harlem, NY which were doing extremely well. They afforded us a very comfortable lifestyle that included private school, the house with a picket fence and a pool out back. Over the next few years, my mom and dad welcomed two more children. My youngest brother and baby sister were the cutest little people. I thought of them as my babies and instantly became their protector.

As the late 70s and early 80s emerged, circumstances in our family dynamics began to change. The financial stability that our family enjoyed began to decline. The income stream that seemed to flow endlessly started to dry up. There were no more nice vacations or parties. My parents could no longer pay for private school. We were able to attend Catholic School because the cost of tuition was more manageable. Finally, they were forced to make the hardest decision of going from homeownership to renting. Had my dad worked with a financial advisor to properly plan and save, I believe he could have sustained his businesses. My dad could have saved more instead of living beyond his means. Investing his money and possibly leveraging a line of credit to get our family through a rough patch may have helped until he was able to come up with another solution. I've learned that there are cycles in life that we all experience - good and bad. This was a bad time for my family, but one that could have been avoided.

Financial knowledge is extremely important to a family's ability to protect their assets and maintain their wealth. Given my level of experience and knowledge now, I

recognize my father's financial downfalls. Here are my top recommendations to protect your assets and plan for your and your family's future:

1) Have estate documents drafted by an attorney
2) Work with a financial advisor and create a financial plan
3) Have an insurance review to determine the amount of life insurance needed to replace any income that may be lost as a result of the head of the household passing away
4) Invest your money for the future - meet with an investment professional for advice
5) Pay off your debt

It was during this time of transition for my family that my parents would argue and actually physically fight. Unfortunately, I have memories of domestic abuse by my father against my mother. Witnessing this abuse made me feel like I had to be responsible for protecting my younger siblings. This is something a young child should not have to think about, but I remember the times like they happened yesterday. Years later I remember asking my mom why she stayed with my dad. She replied that having four young children and not being able to provide for us was her main reason for staying. At that moment, I thought to myself, how sad. I promised myself that I would never be in that position. I would become fiercely independent and would never have to rely on anyone for anything. I am convinced that this is what drove my ambitious attitude - the never give up attitude and the spirit of figuring out how to make things happen when it seems impossible. I knew then even as a young girl that my life was, and still is, about possibilities. I truly believe anything is possible if you are willing to work for it.

As a woman and now a mom myself, I speak about the importance of women being self-sufficient. You have to plan for the future and make sure that you can take care of yourself. One way to do this is by getting your education because knowledge is powerful. Find something that you are passionate about and learn everything you can. Use that knowledge and passion to earn a living. If your employer offers a 401K plan, start participating in it. Save as much and as often as you can on your own. It doesn't require a lot, but it requires consistency over time. This is one of the reasons I volunteer a lot of my time to educating others, especially women, about financial wellness.

- Know your worth and don't be afraid to ask/negotiate for the pay you deserve. Increasing your income allows you to save more.
- Maintain excellent credit by paying your bills on time.
- Purchase a home. Homeownership is a way to create wealth for your family.
- Think about the things you are passionate about and create a plan to start your own business.
- Save, save, save and learn about various ways to diversify your investments.

Eventually, when I was about nine or ten years old, my parents separated for good. We moved in temporarily with my maternal grandmother, Grace, and youngest aunt, Josephine. I remember never wanting to leave my grandmother again. She was the closest person to me on this earth. I truly believe that when my parents moved to White Plains, NY away from the family years prior that they made a huge mistake. Back then the family played a very pivotal role in helping to raise the kids. My dad was away from home a lot and my mother was so young with four children. She needed support and we needed our family altogether.

Nevertheless, my mom finally moved into an apartment near my grandmother's condo. Over the years, we were never too far from my grandmother. At this point we lived in Yonkers, NY and continued attending Catholic school for a time. Yonkers was fun and I remember having so many friends to hang out with. I joined the soccer team and ran track. I was very fast and competed in a lot of competitions. My mom was big on supporting our dreams and encouraged me to compete in pageants, modeling competitions and one day auditioning to sing at the world famous Apollo Theater. My mother was a very creative person and could draw and paint beautifully. She was also the first "fashionista" to influence my love of fashion. My middle and high school years were filled with practice every day after school. I could be found singing, modeling or practicing with the track team.

My siblings and I split our time between our parents' homes for a couple of years. Our dad lived across town and by this time he started working at NBC News at Rockefeller Center in Manhattan. My dad was always brilliant and had become a computer programmer for NBC and later became a manager. However, this was short-lived because he died two years after my parents split. This was a devastating time for our family and for me personally. I vividly remember our mother and grandmother gathering us in the living room to tell us about his passing on the day he died.

I give my mom a lot of credit for never talking bad about our dad. She never discussed the abuse and allowed us to have a relationship with him. During that two-year period we were able to spend a lot of time with him and he really took advantage of the time he had with us. We would wake up to the best banana pancakes. Our dad was a great cook! He taught me how to dance and loved doing "The Hustle" with me. I have some moves on the dance floor because of my dad. We laughed a lot during that time. I loved my father and it

5

was sad that he and my mom could not work out their differences. I could tell when I looked into his eyes that he was sad and missed my mom. He loved her and she loved him, but some people just aren't good for each other.

After our dad passed, we moved to New Jersey with our maternal grandmother. Our mom needed some time to regroup and our grandmother sacrificed to make sure we were taken care of. Two years later, I entered high school which changed my life. My grandmother allowed me to attend high school in Manhattan by using my great grandmother's address. Great grandma had a beautiful apartment near the South Street Seaport not far from Wall Street. I attended Park West High School for one year before the recruiters from Murray Bergtraum came to share information about their business program. I was immediately impressed and applied for admission into the school. It didn't take long for me to find out that I was accepted. Bergtraum - as we called it - had a great reputation and really prepared their students for life in the real world. We had so much talent at Bergtraum. The rap group Jungle Brothers, rapper Q-Tip, actors Damon Wayans, John Leguizamo and many others of influence attended the school. The fashion show was such a big deal and of course, I was in it.

They had a co-op program where students went to school and worked in fortune 500 companies. Students gained real life hands-on experience plus a stipend at the end of the program. I loved it because I was able to get a job on Wall Street at The New York Stock Exchange. My major was accounting and Wall Street was on the list of employers. Technically, students had to be a junior to be in the program. However, I was an excellent student and convinced my teacher to sign-off on my authorization form for acceptance into the program. **This was my first lesson in negotiating for something I wanted. Women should not be afraid to ask for what they want and**

know that they deserve. Men do it all the time and seal the deal with a handshake. Just be prepared to articulate why you deserve what you are asking for. Once I entered the trading floor at The New York Stock Exchange, I made fast friends with all of the brokers and clerks. I had lunch lined up at various firms every day. They didn't know that I was in high school at the time and one firm offered me a permanent position as a clerk typist. Of course I kindly declined, but did accept a summer job. In high school I was making $300.00 per week during the summer.

While the co-op program was a great experience, there is another side to working in a world full of grown men with lots of money and access to anything they desire. Being from uptown and having very savvy parents, I was hip to game. I understood very early on to always protect myself. I ate lunch and even went out to dinner numerous times, but never accepted anything else from these gentlemen. My girlfriends and I were even invited to parties on Fire Island and The Hamptons in Long Island. I had the best times during the summers of 1987 and 1988. However, there were many young women who weren't as aware of their surroundings and were mistreated by some of the same men who extended invitations to me. Unfortunately, many of them left the job due to embarrassment over things they had done. **This is a cautionary tale for young ladies to understand how to value and protect themselves in every situation.**

My time at Murray Bergtraum was invaluable to me. I learned how to type, dress for success, master interview skills, and work in a professional setting at a young age. These are skills that I have been able to expand upon and leverage throughout my career. I have so many fond memories and made some life-long friends from my time in New Jersey and Manhattan.

As I entered my last year of high school, my mother returned to live with us in New Jersey. However, we were older and things had changed. My relationship with my mother was so different that I didn't have a close connection with her anymore. My grandmother decided to move to Virginia and I followed a year after. It was like a culture shock finishing my last year of high school in Petersburg, Virginia. After graduating from Petersburg High School, I attended the local junior college. While attending college, I worked two jobs and got my first apartment. I married my high school sweetheart and we then bought our first home together. Looking back, we were so young and should have waited before getting married. I really believed that I was supposed to marry the man that I loved and wanted to be with no matter how young we were. If I had to do it over, I would have waited until we had time to mature and really figure out what we wanted in life. We separated by our seventh year together and eventually divorced. It was during this time that I also started my career in banking as a teller and volunteering to raise money for various causes. The first fundraising event I attended was a walk for Multiple Sclerosis.

In 1997 I moved to Richmond, VA and a year later was accepted into the management training program at Central Fidelity Bank. This program was a ten month program that provided me with a firm grasp of the various roles within the financial services industry. After the program ended, I went back to the retail side of the bank and became a branch manager. This was **another pivotal period in my life and career. Within a matter of three years, I worked my way up from being a part-time teller to being accepted into a management position.** From there, I went to work in the small business lending unit and eventually landed on the investment team of another local bank. **My team director wanted to include me in the bonus structure because of my hard work and contributions to the team. However,** investment licenses are required in the securities industry. So, the bank paid for the self-study materials and one-by-one, I earned my Series 6, Series 63 and Life & Health licenses. I was able to accomplish this while raising three young children. The knowledge that I gained really changed my perspective on managing money, saving, protecting my credit, and estate planning.

Remarrying and having children of my own helped me really focus on financial planning for my family - something my own parents and many other families do not do. I am not ashamed to admit that I did not know what a trust was at the age of thirty. That same team director made me sit down with one of the trust officers in the bank to set-up a trust for my children. I am forever grateful for his direction and for caring enough to teach me the things that ultimately benefited my family and so many others over the years.

Being a working mom is something that I struggled with for years. I know so many women who feel guilty about being away from their children because they have to work. I truly loved what I was learning at work and the accomplishments that I had made. However, it was an overwhelming feeling at times of guilt because I loved my children, but also wanted a career. For years I pushed my career goals back so that I could be more present with my children as they were growing up. The night before my daughter left for college, we were in her bed talking and I started to cry. I shared my feelings of guilt about working so much during her last few years of high school. She wiped my tears and told me how much of a good mom I was and how proud she was of me. "Mommy," she said, "you are a great mom" and kissed me goodnight. Our kids see the sacrifices we make and they will never forget them.

One of my greatest professional accomplishments is becoming the first African American female Wealth Advisor at my company. I have since gone on to obtain my Series 7, Series 66 and Life & Health licenses while working my way up to becoming a Vice President, Wealth Advisor at one of the largest banks in the country. In this role, my team and I assist high net worth individuals, business owners, busy executives and families with achieving their financial goals. Over the past thirty years, I have been on several diversity counsels, Co-Chaired a business resource group, and joined several boards and women's groups.

It is extremely important to me to continue sharing the knowledge I have gained with women and young girls through workshops and by speaking any chance that I get. I have also worked hard to raise awareness and money to help small, women and minority-owned businesses gain access to capital through my work on the Board of Directors at The Metropolitan Business League, a nonprofit organization.

Through my countless hours of networking and meeting people, I have become very masterful at making great connections in the community. It is through these connections that I have built some wonderful relationships. I am known as the "connector" because I can connect people to other people and resources.

At 51, I am intentional about what I choose to participate in and where I spend my time. I am passionate about creating a pathway for others to follow in my footsteps to do even **more** than what I have been able to accomplish. Along my journey there have been so many good people who mentored me and were advocates for me during my career. **It is important to align yourself with key partners at work, mentors and centers of influence who are willing to help you. Be prepared to participate in new projects because the**

knowledge and experience you gain is invaluable. As I reflect, two people who created a pivotal moment in my career were my previous team director and my partner. These two men believed in my ability and supported me in becoming a Wealth Advisor. When my partner retired, that was a sink or swim moment for me because I had to prove that I was capable of managing our practice by myself. As a result of a supportive team, I proved beyond a doubt that "Yes, I am capable!" This is even more remarkable because as an African American woman, there are very few of us in this position.

Years ago my grandmother Grace would say, "Tani, **you can do more**." **More** is a word that has been a part of my vocabulary since I can remember. I continue to do more and because I give freely, I have been blessed. I have two children who are now young adults in college and one more who will be shortly. They have made me proud because they work just as hard as their mom. Everything that I do, I do with them in mind and have made sure that I do not make the same financial mistakes that my parents made.

A year ago I started my own LLC that I use to purchase real estate as part of my financial plan for the future. This was a personal goal that I set for myself. Start thinking about the things that you would like to accomplish and start crossing them off the list one goal at a time! You are only limited by the amount of time and energy you decide to put into doing the work.

There will be times when fear and self-doubt will be there to greet you. Don't let it stop you from achieving the goals you set for yourself. Push through because the rewards of your hard work are far greater.

God gives everyone a talent. Our job is to understand what that talent is and use it.

11

JoNae', Joseph, Branden and Bryce (my baby who is sleeping in peace), being your Mom has made me the woman I am today. You have made me stronger, wiser, more compassionate and happier knowing you love me unconditionally. I thank my Mom for her passion, generosity and being my biggest cheerleader. My stepdad John is the sweetest and most encouraging. I will always love my Dad, Grandmother and cousin LaTasha who were big influences in my life. My aunt Darlene, aunt Josephine and uncle Ralph were there to help my parents over the years and I am grateful for their love and support. My siblings Melissa, Dax, Earnest and Trina, I love you all so much. Dean, who is my cousin, but more like a brother, thank you for always being there for me. Elon, LaToi, Darnelle, James, Rondelle, Tyrelle, Dax, Jr., Earnest, Jr. Daivon, Shana, Emma, Tee Tee, Nailah, KMario and Keon, I love you all dearly.

My dear Rod, I thank you for being there as I pulled back the layers of my life to help others and in the process helped me to heal.

There are so many family members (too many to name), friends, co-workers and people who have come into my life and blessed me with their love and support. Thank you all for what you have done to help me along my journey!

Acknowledgements

Chi Reed
Noir Beauty
Kizzy.cc46@gmail.com
Facebook: Chi Reed
Instagram: @Hairbychi_rva

Tanya Battle

Tanya presenting an award at a Metropolitan Business League event

Tanya pictured with actors Tim and Daphne Maxwell Reid

Tanya speaking to women about
financial wellness
Photo Credit: Raleigh Marketing

Tanya's children
Photo Credit: Christopher Atkins

MEET TANYA E. BATTLE

As a Wealth Advisor, Tanya and her team provide exceptional personalized service to her clients and their families. With more than 30 years of financial services experience, she has learned the value of truly listening to her clients and providing them with the solutions they need to help address their financial goals. She currently maintains her Series 7, 66 securities registrations and life and health licenses.

During the past 11 years, she has worked alongside her colleagues to provide financial wellness education to women's groups, nonprofit organization members and university students. She serves on the board of directors of the Metropolitan Business League and the Richmond SPCA. She has served with many charitable organizations, including Junior Achievement, The American Heart Walk, The Richmond Food Bank, ChildSavers, Housing Families First, and Community Transformers Foundation.

Disclosure: The views, thoughts and opinions expressed in the text belong solely to the author, and not necessarily to the author's employer, organization, committee or other group or individual.

Connecting to your WOW
Julie Hill

"At the age of 58 you should be thinking about retirement, not starting your own business." WOW – hearing that was tough, but it was a harsh reality that I was forced to overcome. I have always been passionate about creating a space where women in business are accepted and supported. After working in many industries dominated by men, I clawed my way to the top, earning a position in leadership where I could begin to make my mark. I quickly learned that only 33% of small businesses are owned by women. I was determined to help shatter the glass ceiling by helping to provide women with the opportunity to succeed in business creation.

However, it never felt like the right time. I was reliant on my corporate paycheck to get my two children through school and allow my husband to work hard to find a company where he could be happy and our income would be stable. Our primary obstacle for many years was the fear of being without health insurance. Although I was not the happiest, I did what I needed to do. I accepted this to be reality until a wonderful CEO named Tina shared with me the book *One Word that Will Change Your Life* by Gordon, Britton and Page. After reading this book, I was motivated and inspired to focus on change. Seventeen months later, I decided it was time to leave my well-paying job. With laser focus, burning passion, and overwhelming support from family and friends, I decided it was time to take the biggest leap of my life: stepping away from a stable corporate paycheck and embarking on my next journey as an entrepreneur.

Small Town Girl, Big Time Opportunities

The first industry I fell in love with was retail. I loved fashion so after college, I went to work for a retail store in Lynchburg, VA. I was hired as an Assistant Store Manager. One Sunday morning, I received a call from my District Manager. She explained to me that for the next couple of weeks I would be the interim Store Manager. I was super excited for the opportunity, but I wanted to understand what happened to the previous manager. The district manager indicated the old store manager had been stealing merchandise. I was shocked! Having to work twelve-hour days was not fun, but the opportunity was huge! The now ex-store manager would call the store and drive by, claiming I was the person who reported her for stealing. For the record, it wasn't me. I was afraid as to what she might do, so for the safety of my staff and myself, I alerted security about the situation. The ex-store manager found out that I wasn't the one who reported her. She later wrote an apology letter to me.

As life progressed, I continued to work hard, making lasting impressions. I received a call with an opportunity to be an Assistant Manager in Richmond, VA at one of the largest stores in the company. And so, this small town girl was going to the big city! Since the Ashby's Corporate Headquarters was in Richmond, VA, I was very visible when corporate executive leadership would come in. Within a year I was promoted to Interim Store Manager of our Broad Street store, due to our manager's maternity leave. Even after she returned, more opportunities presented themselves. I was approached with yet another huge opportunity when I was asked to move to Orlando, FL, to manage the third largest operation in the retail business. At first, I was hesitant; Richmond was a quick couple of hours ride home, but Orlando, on the other hand, seemed like a whole new world! I knew what I needed to do to continue my growth with the company, so I packed up my bags and headed to sunny Florida!

Unfortunate events and better days ahead

As a twenty-three-year-old, Orlando was the place to be. Not only was my training going well, but I was experiencing new things and creating lifelong connections. Time really does fly when you are having fun. Six months later, I was turning twenty-four the next day. But on this particular night, at 11:00 pm, I received a call. Usually, I would not be awake at this hour, but I had scheduled the day off for some much-needed rest and relaxation. I answered the phone and immediately sensed the uneasiness through the line. The next minutes were a blur as my father explained to me that my younger sister, Susan, had been killed by a drunk driver. She was only 16 years old. Without thinking, I packed my bags and booked the first flight back to Virginia. After the funeral, it became clear to me that I needed to be back in Virginia to provide support for my parents and two younger siblings.

My hopes and prayers were quickly answered. I received an offer from Talbots as the Store Manager at the Massachusetts Avenue Store in Washington, DC. I had the most unbelievable encounters in that position. I had the opportunities to dress Supreme Court Justice Sandra Day O'Conner and other high level government officials. One day, soon to be First Lady Barbara Bush and her large security detail entered my store. She was delightful and kind, but attempting to treat her as any other customer while surrounded by six large men, was daunting. I helped her pick out a new swimsuit, a cover up and several other items for her trip to Camp David...wow, what a day!

When the local media caught wind of my encounter, I received a phone call from one of the National Morning shows wanting to interview me regarding my time with the future First Lady. I quickly called the Corporate Office, and it was decided that I, along with the Regional Manager, would be interviewed. I was so nervous that I gave myself a bad case of laryngitis.

Back to Virginia - Growing a Family and Making Connections

I was thankful Talbot's provided the opportunity on Massachusetts Ave, but the hours were long, and I was looking for a change in pace. After six months in DC, I was promoted again – this time as the new Training Store Manager at River Road in Richmond. I was thankful to be back in a familiar town with existing friendships. In my twenties, I dated but being career focused caused many of those relationships to take a backseat to my career goals. A mutual friend wanted to set me up on a blind date; typically, I would've said no, but for some reason, this one felt different. That man would end up being my future husband. Hollywood whirlwind romances had nothing on us. After meeting in June, it did not take long for us to realize this one was meant to be. We were married the next September. I was truly blessed. I had a wonderful husband, a great job and just nine months later, we were pregnant with our first child.

My pregnancy started out great, but at about 20 weeks I began to have complications, including high blood pressure, but the size of our son's head in utero was the greatest concern. My husband traveled frequently for his job, so he was out of town on the day of my specialist visit. The physician immediately began speaking to me, explaining that the size of my son's head could indicate a possible diagnosis of Down Syndrome or hydrocephalus. He began to discuss options, but I was too overwhelmed by all the information and emotions. Even though I was mid breakdown, I gathered myself enough to leave. I drove directly to my husband in Charlottesville, VA. This was before the days of cell phones. Even though he knew I was coming, he had no idea of the conversation I had had with the physician. We elected to undergo the dangerous but informational amniocentesis testing. Thankfully, when the results came in, our son happened to be in perfect health. In April of 1993, we welcomed our son three weeks early, weighing nine pounds, eleven ounces and twenty-two inches long.

A couple years later, after adding a daughter to our family and returning from maternity leave, I was approached by a gentleman named George representing the Retail Merchants Association. Though he was a stranger then, I would later call him a close friend and mentor. We connected at a baseball game sponsored by the Association. He was immediately impressed with my knowledge and go-getter attitude. Through his strong recommendation, I was hired as the Director of Membership. This role was different than anything I had held before. I was able to mold and build my skill sets. I thought this was my dream job in a new industry, working with a Retail nonprofit association.

I knew that I needed to join VSAE and ASE, the industry specific statewide and national associations. Both organizations provided great continuing education that would later help with my advancement in the association. In my time at Retail Merchants', I developed a referral program bringing over 200 new members into the association. I then created a sponsorship and vendor program that would generate major capital for the association. I had been so successful in this position that when our previous CEO retired, I was asked to apply for the position.

Important tip: Strongly recommended to join both National and local organizations to broaden your network.

Unfortunately, at this time, my husband also received a promotion, and our family was making the move to Fredericksburg, a town an hour north. While it was difficult to turn down such an amazing opportunity, I knew I would not be able to commit the time and effort required. The board selected a new CEO.. After she began her new role, she named me the VP of Membership and soon there would be three very strong minded, confident female executive leaders in the organization. Although good, this would prove to be a challenge. To encourage growth, we decided that a **business coach** would be a great idea for all of us. My first time meeting with her, I was reluctant and guarded. We completed a personality test that ultimately provided me with a sense of direction.

Continuing to strengthen my leadership skills, we were recommended to read and take the Strengthsfinder assessment. This provided my top five strengths which were Focus, Maximizer, Command, Significance and Realtor. These words made me curious about other opportunities that might be out there that I have yet to discover. One of my members encouraged me to meet with the new CEO and Chief Marketing Officer of Eastern Virginia Bank Shares. While at an event, the CEO approached me with an interesting offer. He explained that he was looking for a Senior Vice President of a new women's program named P.O.W.E.R. I was hesitant because I had never held a job in banking. He still encouraged me to apply because he was confident that I would be the perfect fit for this position. After 19 years at Retail Merchants', I began my newest chapter and I began broadening my professional network.

Banking - New Opportunity in a New Industry

P.O.W.E.R. (Potential of Women's Enterprisers Realized) was thought up by the CEO to help encourage the connection and networking of women in business. Over the next six years we would trademark the program and would work with bank managers, commercial lenders, and bank partners to create a program that extended far beyond the traditional scope of banking. Instead, it was about building a network devoted to connecting and supporting female entrepreneurs and women. In my time at EVB and SONA, we recruited over 2,000 customers and generated millions of dollars in deposits. The P.O.W.E.R. program spread like wildfire as we expanded our network to cover all of Virginia and Maryland.

Important Tip: When developing a program or a product you should work through the Trademarking process in the early stages of development.

When Covid hit, we were forced to rethink our platform due to growing health concerns. We had to get creative. We put more time in expanding our social media presence, putting all our information and resources at customers' fingertips. Our social media quickly gained popularity, increasing in likes and shares overnight. We wanted to showcase our members and employees by creating a podcast. This platform ended up reaching hundreds of listeners, which generated additional revenue and attention for POWER.

Important Tip: Continue to develop a strong social and marketing strategy.

Around this time, the CEO, the man who had birthed the idea of P.O.W.E.R., announced he would be retiring and a new CEO was appointed. From the beginning, the new CEO made his intentions to change the women's program clear. Our team quickly became frustrated because we spent many hours building and growing this program.

Before we knew it, P.O.W.E.R. was a thing of the past or it would look different. The program quickly dissolved and took its new direction. I received a call from the bank CEO that he wanted me to help create a new program focused on integrating single mothers into the workforce by creating a training program to teach necessary skills and working with non-profit organizations to provide work opportunities. We began the program with an introductory class of five single mothers. After five months of rigorous training and education, three out of the five graduated. The CEO was thrilled. The next step was to place the single mothers in banking departments Monday through Thursday. On Fridays, we hosted professional speakers which included representatives from organizations like Dress for Success Central Virginia. I asked Holly Byrd Miller to lead this effort and she did an amazing job. We also had budget classes, LinkedIn training, developing your 60-second elevator speech, banking educational class, plus the women attended a Women's Conference and engaged in a community project. I was so proud that my banking partners worked together to make this a success. I then asked three other bank employees to help interview for the next class. We had a great response. We had six single moms starting and we were all excited about these new interns.

This new position was fulfilling, but I continued to feel like something was missing because of my passion for working with women entrepreneurs and women in business. I continued to long for the feeling that I got when creating connections with P.O.W.E.R. After many discussions, I decided that we wanted to continue the services and opportunities provided by P.O.W.E.R. My partners and I decided to test the waters by offering our marketing expertise to a few small businesses with which we had made prior connections. We began small by taking on marketing projects for a carwash, a jewelry store, and a non-profit organization.

While still working our full-time jobs, we worked on the projects at night and on the weekends. The feedback we received from our initial customers encouraged us to continue this path, adding additional services in business development, marketing and financial.

Important Tip: Create diverse focus groups when starting a business of trusting advisors. Also, make sure that you have developed a WOW team that works together for the success of your business 1)Business attorney 2)Banker 3)CPA/ Bookkeeper 4)Business Coach.

My husband's career had moved him back to Richmond, but due to our ties to Fredericksburg, we both continued to make the hour commute. However, during COVID, my husband and I came to the profound realization that it was time that we prioritized our mental health and well-being. We decided to make the move back to Richmond. Within one day on the market, our house received multiple offers and we sold. In all the excitement, we failed to realize that this would ultimately leave us homeless. Thankfully, we were able to move in temporarily with some close friends until we were able to find our perfect forever home.

Our relocation provided me with the time to invest in my own personal experiences and growth. I joined Business Networking International, a group dedicated to providing a platform for connection and creating referrals for businesses worldwide. I attended weekly Thursday morning virtual meetings and created relationships with over 25 other business owners. Months later, we were finally back heading towards our new sense of normal. Our bank reopened the lobbies and we were given the green light to begin meeting in person again.

While at a quarterly training, I was introduced to a book that would create a spark and provide the focus and determination that I needed. The book is titled *One Word That Will Change Your Life* written by Jon Gordon, Dan Britton and Jimmy Page. It truly caused me to begin thinking about my life and the direction I desired to go. My word was FOCUS. This word started a chain of events that would set the course of my next year. Inspired, I shared this book with my partners. Within months, we decided to put our spin on a new women's organization.

June 17, 2022 was my last day in banking. I provided a 30-day notice and I have never been happier. My connections, my passion, the support from family and friends, but most of all, my faith in God has provided me with breadcrumbs and made me hunger for this journey with Women that are On their Way (WOW). The WOW Collaborative was born with over 40 plus members and with many marketing projects.

Important Tip: When securing your financial readiness, pay off credit card debt, apply for a line of credit, build savings and cash reserves, and work with a financial planner.

So, this has been my journey, my road to success. But something I am often reluctant to share is that during my time at Retail Merchants, I found myself in the biggest battle of my life. My health was declining. After many years of pain, testing and many doctors' visits, I was diagnosed with Interstitial cystitis. It is a syndrome where basically, my bladder died. It was determined that it needed to be removed to improve my quality of life. I also suffer from kidney disease and kidney stones. Due to my complicated health history, it has led to many scary infections. However, through adversity comes opportunity. I have created connections with many organizations and am now an active board member of the

National Kidney Association, dedicated to raising awareness and, hopefully, improving the lives of the many individuals who suffer from kidney disease.

Important Tip: Always prioritize your health.

If that small-town girl from Altavista, Virginia saw me today, she would be overcome with pride. I have worked my way from the ground up, overcoming adversity and breaking barriers. I have built a unique network of women in business that I will continue to grow and mold. With laser focus, burning passion and overwhelming support from family and friends, I am now the creator of opportunities and the Co-Founder of The WOW Collaborative.

Julie Hill

Julie pictured with her family

MEET JULIE HILL

Julie Hill is the Co-Founder and Creator of Opportunities for The WOW Collaborative. Her professional experience includes seven years as the Senior VP of Primis, a $3.09 billion regional bank headquartered in Glen Allen, VA and 19 years as VP of Business Development with Retail Merchants Association in Richmond, VA. Known as an all-star connector, Julie focuses on connecting women in business as well as nonprofits to help clients and prospects navigate the business environment.

Acknowledgements

Quinn Hill
Terri Drewry
Chesterfield County Schools
Instagram: @scoutieboy1408

Laura Gaythwaite
Cornerstone Strategic Alliance
Website: www.cssa.pro
LinkedIn: Laura Gaythwaite

Kristy Geiger
Eventive Thinking and Kristy Geiger Real Estate
Website: www.eventivethinking.com , www.kristygeiger.com
Facebook: @eventivethinking , @kristygeigerrealtor
Instagram: @eventivethinking , @kristygeigerrealtor
LinkedIn: Kristy Archer Geiger

Nancy Foster
Virginia Asset Management
Nancy.foster@vamllc.com

Andrea Hamilton
Facebook: Andrea Campbell Hamilton
Instagram: Andrea Campbell Hamilton
LinkedIn: Andrea Campbell Hamilton

Page Bethke
The Promo Department, LLC
Website: thepromodepartment.com
Facebook: @ThePromoDepartment
Instagram: @thepromodepartment.com
LinkedIn: Page Bethke

Susan Hingst

Glacier View Golf Club
Website: GlacierView Golf.com
Instagram: @Glacier.view.golf.club

Joe Shearin
The WOW Collaborative
Facebook: Joe Shearin
LinkedIn: Joe Shearin

Emilee Johnson

Michelle Simon
The WOW Collaborative
www.thewowcollaborative.com
Facebook: @thewowcollaborative.com
LinkedIn: Michelle Hastings Simon

GO GET IT
Reba Hollingsworth

I will never forget this particular day. I was checking out at Trader Joe's after work. Before the cashier finished scanning, I went to grab my debit card. I couldn't find it. I was having a mini panic attack at cash register #6. The other two credit cards in my wallet were maxed out. I had twenty dollars, but it wasn't enough to cover my few items. The line was growing and I was praying no one recognized me. I'm flustered and desperately scouring my purse to find that card before the cashier hits the total amount. Too late. I literally began putting some items back. I'm embarrassed. I'm a TV news anchor and couldn't pay for my own groceries. Back in my car and with tears in my eyes, I ask the question I've been avoiding for months: "Is starting a business from the ground up - especially during a divorce - the biggest mistake I've ever made?" I had some soul searching to do as a journalist, an entrepreneur, a mom and a soon-to-be divorcee.

At age seven, I knew I wanted to be on TV. It was mesmerizing to watch Talk Show Host Phil Donahue running up and down the aisle with a microphone in his hand. When Oprah came on the scene, it changed everything for this little chocolate girl in Texas seeing her very own possibilities come to life.

Alief Elsik High School in Houston is where I got my first taste of journalism while writing for the school's newspaper. When I got to college as a broadcast journalism major at

Southwest Texas State University in San Marcos, I was even more addicted to writing "the news". As I got closer to graduation, I felt prepared to get a job in TV. I could write, conduct interviews, shoot videos and edit. I was ready to take on the world of TV news, but no one told the world.

Feeling crushed, I went back home to Houston. I couldn't find a TV job for eighteen long months. It was humbling. My job search consisted of calling small market TV stations to see if they had any openings. These were the days before the internet. I mailed out countless paper resumes and clunky ¾ inch video tapes showing the news stories I put together at school and during my internship at KXAN in Austin. These days, sending out resume tapes is a whole lot easier and looks a lot more polished compared to my outdated resume. Now, you can just send a link of your work via email or social media. Either way, the goal is still the same. You cross your fingers that the news director will watch the first few minutes of your resume tape before stopping it. I remember doing a follow-up call to a news director at a small TV station in Louisiana to see if he watched my tape. He said, "You weren't even one of my top candidates. Maybe you should think about doing something else." All of these years later, I've never forgotten those words. After that soul crushing call, I told my mother I was going to find a job so I could start making money. She responded in her no-nonsense tone, "We sent you to school to have a career; not just to make money. If you want a job in TV, **GO GET IT**."

After a little motivation from mama, I randomly wrote to KTRK news anchor, Gina Gaston, for advice. Early one morning (she was a morning anchor at the time), she called and said, "You are too comfortable. You need to get in your car and drive to these TV stations. You need to show your face." Advice taken! My dad and I drove to just about every small market TV station in Texas and Louisiana - and that's how I landed my first job.

I was hired as an anchor-reporter in Victoria, Texas making $12,000 a year. I had a college degree, but desperately needed the experience. When I speak to young students and journalists today, I tell them that **opportunity and money are not always synonymous**. Sometimes in the beginning, it's about getting in, learning your craft and moving on. However, I can testify that the struggle was definitely real.

Nine months later, my next opportunity came knocking as a weekend anchor position in Abilene, Texas. It was a position I didn't apply for, but they remembered me from my "job tour" with my dad. I started my new job making $16,000. Again, the experience was invaluable. It was there that I began working on my "news voice". I had to learn to slow down my delivery and I was consistently leaving the "g" off "ing" words. And viewers didn't mind letting me know either. I was saying words like cookin', workin', playin'. You get the point. With what little money I was making, I paid for voice lessons which were one of the best investments I've made for my career. **Whatever your profession, making the investment to sharpen your skills will always pay off.** I was eventually promoted to main anchor which was rare for a young black woman in small town Abilene. It was there I started to build my confidence as an anchor and as a journalist. I worked with a group of people who wanted to see me grow and succeed. To this day, they are still my dearest friends. After five years though, I was ready to move on.

In 2000, I specifically targeted Richmond, Virginia, a medium sized market, for my next job because my fiancé' got accepted to law school nearby. Remembering Gina Gaston's advice to step out of my comfort zone, I met with two news directors in Richmond. My meeting at WTVR felt different. The news director wanted me to meet the General Manager, Mark Pimentel. Why did that name sound so familiar? When I left his office, I realized Mark called me months prior asking for a resume tape. At the time, he was at a station in Alabama. I had my sights on Virginia, not Alabama, so I had blown him off. Realizing how bad this looked, I called Mark and asked if he remembered me. He said "I remembered you the moment you walked into my office." I was upfront and apologized for dissing him and then explained why I wanted to come to Richmond and was hired that week. **This was my first lesson in not burning bridges.** The world is small. The world of TV news is even smaller.

I left Abilene and started in Richmond as morning reporter and was then eventually promoted to morning anchor. Richmond was on another level for me both professionally and personally. It was the perfect career move, but it was also time for a new change after five years. By this time I was married and became a freelance reporter in DC and Baltimore working at news stations and bureaus such as CNN Newsource. I thought working at CNN would fulfill my dream of working network news; however, it turned out not to be a good fit for either of us. From that experience, **I learned to give myself permission to change my mind with no regrets.** After four years in the DC area and as a new mom, I was really missing Richmond. I called. I asked. And I was back on the morning anchor desk. Boy, I'm glad I didn't burn that bridge.

Life was good in Richmond….for a moment. In 2010, my parents came to visit for the holidays and my mother suddenly died on Christmas Eve. I was heartbroken and numb. My grandmother died days later. I believe she died of a broken heart. Two of the strongest forces and voices in my life were gone. The heartache didn't seem to stop. In 2015, my best friend, Stephanie, died of cancer. Stephanie was the evening anchor at WTVR. She was like my own sister. To add to my world of sadness, my marriage was beginning to unravel. Those monumental losses changed me and how I saw my life. Professionally, I was in a good place. Our morning news team received four regional Emmy Awards and I was teaching broadcast writing at Virginia Commonwealth University. On paper, I looked like a success story, but I kept feeling this overwhelming sense that I was destined for more. It felt like a higher power was speaking to me.

For years, I'd dreamed of being an entrepreneur. Something about creating and owning my own business felt powerful and alluring, but I had never pursued it. Maybe I was scared. In the midst of my fear, I was reminded of my grandmother. Even with a limited education, she was a successful entrepreneur. She made custom drapes for clients in Dallas. My grandfather would help her with jobs. I have vivid memories as a child tagging along and watching her in action. She was my first entrepreneurial role model.

An intense nudge came in 2017 when an idea fell quite literally into my lap. Each morning as a news anchor, I dreaded and complained about putting on my wireless microphone whenever I was wearing a dress. It required unzipping my dress and struggling to attach the bulky microphone onto my bra strap and praying the zipper wouldn't break. It was a frustrating process that I went through daily, along with countless other women in TV news. We've attached microphones to headbands, ACE bandages, Velcro straps or the sleeve of a sweatshirt. I knew I could create a more sophisticated solution. I'm not going to lie; I had a lot of doubts about turning a simple idea into a full-fledged business. I've been a journalist for almost 30 years. Starting a new business from scratch was unfamiliar and scary territory.

I sent my seamstress, Herena, a picture of my friend securing her microphone with a bandage. I wanted to create something similar, but with a stretchy fabric and other features. I also had to work on the business side. I set up Pink Unicorn, LLC and my dear friend Elizabeth, a professional naming consultant, helped me explore potential product names. One day, the expression "aha moment" – one of Oprah's favorite phrases – lit up in my head like a lightbulb. That's it! "AHA Wrap"! I felt even more confident with the name choice when I drove to work the next day and the song on the radio was an old 80s hit called "Take On Me," by the band – you guessed it – A-ha. (I call that a "God wink"!)

A couple bits of advice when creating a product: protect yourself. *Carefully go through the trademark and patent processes with the concept, design, name, and logo. If someone offers to help with your project, even on a pro-bono basis, create a written agreement before you get started to make sure you both have a clear understanding of expectations during and after the project. Seeking the advice of a small business attorney could be beneficial.*

As Herena and I tested prototypes for the AHA Wrap, I solicited the advice of some female TV News friends. My co-worker Tracy suggested snaps. We added the snaps and four different sizes, but the wrap was still falling down. I could never put a "falling" wrap on the market.

In February 2018, Tracy introduced me to another entrepreneur, Michelle. One day at Michelle's house, I told her about the issues I was having with the wrap falling down. Michelle went into her bedroom and came out holding a tennis skirt and said, "maybe you need something like this" as she pointed to the silicone elastic. Another "aha moment"! Silicone elastic is used in women's clothing to keep things in place. It would be the perfect solution for my AHA Wrap!

Michelle introduced me to Stacy and Rachel who had mass-produced their own product. They gave me the scoop on how to find a factory and use a forwarding company to ship my goods. By mid-summer, the prototype was ready to go. In order to pay for production and shipping, I took out a loan from my 401K. Let me be clear on this point: I wouldn't recommend tapping into your 401K, but it was the quickest solution for me. **If you need to fund your startup, consider a bank loan (which is not the easiest to get if you're just starting out), a small business loan through your state government, crowdfunding, an investor or a business organization that fosters the development of small businesses.** I didn't receive any outside financial help, but I was blown away by the number of people willing to help me launch my new business. My friend Madeline created the website. Jason, a news photographer, shot the pictures and video for marketing and advertising. Friends Candace, Wendy, Kelly and Amie modeled for those pictures and Claudia, a reporter-friend, modeled for the logo. A conversation at my daughter's bus stop led me to Liz, who became my monogrammer for customizing the AHA Wraps.

Another tip: If you're thinking about becoming an entrepreneur, consider the resources around you and tap into your own personal network of expertise. *Entrepreneurs can't do it alone. I'm forever thankful for the advice, guidance, and support I received from numerous people – many of whom are women! They want me to succeed as much as I want to see them thrive and shine.*

AHA Wrap launched November 14, 2018 and I had only one sale and it was from my good friend, Shelby. Initially, some customers criticized the $30/$40 price tag, but I'm a strong believer in not lowering your price in hopes of getting more sales. It's a tempting temporary fix, but ultimately **people will pay for quality**. With that said, my initial sales were extremely slow and I was hemorrhaging money. Paying for a divorce attorney, childcare, household bills and now a start-up were impacting my financial security in a big way. Stepping out of my "comfort zone" was starting to feel really uncomfortable. Despite the uneasy feeling, I knew there's no such thing as a "perfect" time to start a business. Life will always get in the way. As my church Pastor would say: The Miracle is in the Mess. Amen.

In November of 2021, TRI V3RSA hit the market— a 3-in-1, vegan leather, gender neutral messenger bag. Just like the AHA Wrap, I wanted to create a product to make people's lives easier.

With both products, the business is growing thanks to pop-ups, word-of-mouth, friends, quality products and social media. I made another investment to hire a social media whiz. That was a big weight off my shoulders. Kristina posts content consistently and sends out monthly newsletters. Running your social media platforms is a job in itself! **Hiring a social media expert is a worthy investment that will free you to concentrate on the business**.

With the AHA Wrap, newsroom bosses are buying in bulk for their female news talent and it's expanding beyond TV. Other industries are using the AHA WRAP: public speakers, ministers, politicians, along with audio visual companies and journalism schools. I couldn't be prouder, but I still see and strive for BIGGER. That nudge is always there.

Creating a business is bigger than me. I'm not only building a new life, but a legacy. It's a legacy I can pass on to my daughter, fellow entrepreneurs and Girl Bosses. It may not seem like it sometimes, but our girls—in particular—are watching. We are passing down more than possible generational wealth. **We are passing down strength,**

autonomy, and ability to carve out our own place in the world.

Over the past two decades, the number of entrepreneurs has increased by 114% (INC). Women of color are the fastest growing group of entrepreneurs. According to the Bureau of Labor Statistics, one of the top reasons businesses fail within the first five years is cash-flow, lack of capital. We all play a vital role in helping these small businesses, these big ideas, succeed.

I'm committed to my legacy of being a staunch supporter, cheerleader, and ally for other business owners. How do I do that? First, by sharing my story. Just like how other women shared their story with me. Knowledge is power. What I know about starting and operating a business helps no one if I keep it a secret. That knowledge has the power to trickle down to other new business owners. Secondly, I can offer my support. I can financially support small businesses as a customer. I can also support with a simple email, card, or text that says "I see you. Keep up the great work!" I can't stress this enough: we need each other.

As an entrepreneur, the doubts, disappointments, and second guessing can run deep. However, there are abundant rewards. We can use all of it—the good and not-so-good, to push and propel us to our greater purpose.

Back to my earlier question: "Is starting a business during a divorce the biggest mistake I ever made?" Absolutely not! It's probably one of the smartest decisions I ever made. Divorce wasn't my ending; it was my rebirth. I ended one thing and started another. And by birthing new things into the world that could help me and others, I saw my own self-worth in a whole new way. I had yet another AHA moment: I finally felt my gut feeling and my faith intersect. And if you find yourself at the same crossroad, contemplating your own life changing move, keep the words of my mother in your mind: **GO GET IT!**

Reba speaking at a Metropolitan Business League event
Photo Credit: ImagesByKecia, LLC

Miss America 2020, Camille Schrier, wearing her AHA Wrap

Model Brittani with TRI V3RSA bag
Photo Credit: Emmanuel Pezoa

MEET REBA HOLLINGSWORTH

Reba Hollingsworth is a 4-time Emmy Award Winning TV News Journalist. In her 25-plus year career in the television news industry, Reba has covered stories from the local courthouse to the White House. Reba's long TV career has led her down the path of entrepreneurship. She's the creator of the AHA Wrap and TRI V3RSA bag - two stylish products with the purpose of making the lives of people easier.

Reba Hollingsworth

Reba was born and raised in Texas. She graduated with a degree in broadcast journalism from Southwest Texas State University (currently known as Texas State University) in San Marcos. She began her TV news career in the small Texas town of Victoria at KAVU-TV. Nine months later, Reba became weekend anchor at KTXS-TV in Abilene and was quickly promoted to main anchor. Five years later, Reba accepted a morning reporter position at WTVR-TV in Richmond, Virginia. Again, she was promoted quickly to morning anchor. After five years in Richmond, Reba became a freelance reporter in the DC area working for FOX 5 in DC, WBAL in Baltimore, Hearst DC bureau, and CNN Newsource. In 2009, Reba returned to the highly rated morning show at WTVR-TV and received four regional Emmy awards for the morning newscasts. She's also received distinguished awards for her breast cancer awareness stories. Reba brought her skills and knowledge to the classroom as an adjunct professor teaching broadcast writing at Virginia Commonwealth University. Beyond her TV job, Reba is deeply invested and involved in the community she serves.

In 2018, Reba stepped out on faith and pursued her entrepreneurial dreams by creating the AHA Wrap for television news women. The stylish leg wrap holds the wireless microphone for women wearing a dress. The AHA Wrap is sold across the nation from its website and Amazon. Three years later, Reba channeled TV women again by creating the TRI V3RSA bag. However, the convertible bag goes beyond women in TV. It's the 3-in-1 bag for your life.

Reba stays busy as a journalist and entrepreneur, but the center of her world is her daughter, Jillian. Reba is a member of The Metropolitan Business League, National Association of Black Journalists and Alpha Kappa Alpha Sorority, Incorporated.

Keep in touch with Reba:
Instagram: @RebaOnTv | LinkedIn: Reba Hollingsworth
Website: www.ahawrap.com

Acknowledgements

Carrie Brunner
Instagram: @carrie_r_brunner
LinkedIn: Carrie Brunner

Pamela Harris Cox
Granted Media Productions, LLC
Website: Pamela-Cox.com
Instagram: @Granted100
LinkedIn: Pamela Harris Cox

Christy Burton Omarzai
Argyle
Website: www.LoveArgyle.com
Facebook: @ChristyBurtonOmarzai
Instagram: @ChristyOmarzai
LinkedIn: Christy Burton Omarzai

Nicole Jackson

Marlene Fuller
LEAP: Live Empowered With An Awakened Purpose, LLC
Website: Marlenefuller.com
Facebook: LeapwithDrMarlene
Instagram: @DrMarleneFuller
LinkedIn: DrMarleneFuller

Dr. Tamika S. Hood
Couture Coaching by Dr. Tamika S. Hood
Website: www.tamikashood.com
Facebook: @TamikaSHood
Instagram: @dr.tamika_s.hood
LinkedIn: Dr. Tamika S. Hood Ph.D., ICF-PCC, CPDC, PHR, SHRM-CP

Michele Wilson
Ma'Michele's Cafe
Website: www.mamicheles.com
Facebook: @mamichelescafe
Instagram: @mamicheles
LinkedIn: Chef Michele Wilson

Kevin Fox
The Suited Fox
www.thesuitedfox.com
Facebook: @thesuitedfox.com
Instagram: @TheSuitedFox
LinkedIn: Kevin Fox

Brandi Johnson

Lisa Gwaltney
Facebook: @lisa.gwaltney.9
LinkedIn: Lisa Gwaltney

Andrea Starr Forward
Foundation VA
Website: forwardfoundationva.org
Facebook:@forwardfoundationva
Instagram: @forwardfoundation_va
LinkedIn: Andrea (Mandel) Starr and Forward Foundation VA

Coletti
Colettis Hair Salon
Website: Colettistarks.webs.com
Facebook: @Colettistarksbrown
Instagram: @Coletti_starks_brown

Faizah Hough
Alabaster Advocacy Group

Website: www.alabasteradvocacy.org
Facebook: @alabasteradvocacy
Instagram: @alabasteradvocacy
LinkedIn: Faizah Hough

Barry Farmer
Website: www.BarryFarmer.com
Instagram: @iambarryfarmer

Gina Burgin
LinkedIn: Gina Burgin

Tarra L. Pressey
FYZICAL Therapy & Balance Centers Short Pump
Website: fyzical.com/short-pump-va

Kim Martin
KLM Scholarship Foundation
www.KLMFoundation.org
Facebook: @klmscholarshipfoundation
Instagram: @klmsf
LinkedIn: KLM Scholarship Foundation

Kennetra Pulliams
LinkedIn: @KPulliams

Sharon Oliver
The Creatives Playground
Creativesplaygroundrva.com
Facebook: Sharon Oliver
Instagram: @Sharonolivertv

Shelby Brown
Shelby Brown Media Solutions
Website: www.ShelbyBrownNbiz.com
Facebook: @shelbybrownmediasolutions

Reba Hollingsworth

Instagram: @shelbybrownmediasolutions
LinkedIn: Shelby Brown Media Solutions

Entrepreneurs are Unicorns

Catina Jones

When I hear the name Otis Daniel Hawkins, Sr., it reminds me of, coupled with God, a lifetime of motivation and inspiration for my success. You see, my father grew up in the civil rights era, and like most men of his time, served in the Vietnam War. He earned the Military Order of the Purple Heart for his service then returned home to serve his community and to inspire others. My father saw no failure in trying new ventures. That's probably why I see no ceilings.

Upon returning home from service, my dad worked at the local hospital then went on to work at a menswear store. His "aha" moment came during a promotion, but that promotion was not for him. As a manager, he was training a white employee to work at the store as a supervisor. That person got the promotion, not my dad. It was a hard lesson, well learned, and the last time he worked at a company he did not own. This opened my eyes to the road less traveled: entrepreneurship. I was very young when my dad started his first of (eventually) three businesses and I remember them all fondly.

The first business, ironically, was a men's shop – not to compete with his former employer, but because he was enthused with fashion and being well-dressed. His slacks were always creased down the middle. His suits were tailored and his Stacy Adams shoes always shined. His next venture was a yogurt shop called 'It's Only Natural.' His final success was Richmond Alert Security Systems. The company slogan, though attractive for the industry, applies to entrepreneurship as a whole: "If it's worth having, it's worth protecting." He owned Richmond Alert Security for 30 years. His business was widely known and respected around Richmond with several clients being friends, family, and former classmates. He owned and maintained this business until his passing in 2011.

Ultimately, my father knew he wanted to provide for his family on his own terms. He always encouraged my siblings and me to have our own by working for ourselves. For him, as a Black man, entrepreneurship was the epitome of freedom. After growing up in the segregated South, serving in the military, and even being overlooked by a former employer, my father recognized his strength and power in entrepreneurship. How could I not be inspired growing up under that?

I'd say entrepreneurs are unicorns. Not everyone has what it takes to be a business owner and there's nothing wrong with that. No leader is successful without a team to help execute her vision and build upon her dream. It takes an immeasurable amount of faith, and some may say insanity, to walk away from a secure career that includes guaranteed benefits, a retirement plan, 401K, a consistent salary and other benefits, to say "okay, I'm going to work for myself." As an entrepreneur, you must be ready to bet on yourself every day and ready to take unknown risks. I'd be lying if I said it would be easy. But is it worth it? Definitely.

A Faith-Based Compass

"We've come this far by faith, leaning on the Lord…trusting in His Holy Word…He's never failed me yet," is one of the many gospel songs from my childhood that has carried me this far in my journey. Faith is the cornerstone of my family's foundation. My father and grandfather were pastors, along with cousins, aunts, and uncles who held roles in the church. No meal was consumed without grace, and no accolade was acknowledged without, "First giving honor to God..." I slide this phrase in so swiftly whenever I give praise because this upbringing is crucial to who I am today and the path I lead.

I had a faith-based foundation early on in my childhood. Knowing God provided me a spiritual compass, a moral code to live by. I knew there was a stronger, wiser, and all-knowing source looking over me. It truly helped during hard times. Even when I was unsure about a certain decision, I was sure there was someone higher guiding my life. In essence, having faith is like having a compass; it gives direction. Though I may go the wrong way or feel lost, my faith brings me back on the right path. Scriptures that guide my spiritual compass include Philippians 4:13, "I can do all things through Christ who strengthens me." Also 2 Timothy 1:7, "For God has not given us a spirit of fear, but of power, and of love, and of a sound mind."

At this point in my life, my faith is an essential part of me. I cannot speak without mentioning God's goodness, because this all started with a promise unto Him. I told God that if I am successful in this industry, if anyone ever asked me how so, I would be faithful to give Him all the glory. With every deal secured, speaking engagement booked, award accepted, training completed, or coaching session led, I give Him thanks. For without Him, there would be no Catina Jones and there would be no success. These pages would be blank.

Entrepreneurship is a faith-based walk. There are resources to help make the work easier, but at the end of *each* day, it boils down to the decisions you make. You must exercise faith with whom you have in your circle, the offers you accept or decline, and the relationships you build. Sometimes no matter where you turn, there is no answer or insight, you just lean on faith. That's where trusting in God is monumentally crucial. No matter how much experience I have, nothing is possible without God. Period!

It Doesn't Happen Overnight...or the Next Day, but in Perfect Timing.

My road to entrepreneurship was impacted by my father, but also my journey in life. He and my mother knew I was smart, savvy, and, would one way or another, have my way. I guess you could call that determination. I started my career at a bank and worked my way up the corporate ladder. I began at the most entry-level position with keying checks. After a few years and multiple promotions, I was managing sales and relationships of large corporate accounts. Around this time, I was a young 20-something woman and married with children. Though my career trajectory was on the up and up, my father never encouraged me to get comfortable with the "stability" a job brought. Employees know yearly what their salary will be. There's a limit. With entrepreneurship, there is no limit. At this time, my husband was the breadwinner in the household. With my third child, I decided to be a stay-at-home mother. We couldn't afford to cover daycare for three children and with him earning more, I was fine stepping away from work.

You're probably wondering where my college experience comes in. It doesn't. I knew after high school that I wanted to start my career. College did not interest me. It's not for everyone and isn't the only route to success. I did take a few business courses at a community college, but when my children came, my priorities shifted. In hindsight, my career in corporate America was my *college*. I learned crucial skills that have been pivotal in my success, including networking, customer service, maintaining relationships, and other business skills I use today.

My company, ICON Realty Group, did not happen overnight. I started my real estate journey as an independent contractor. I led a team of about ten people. Immediately, I was a top producer. I received nearly every award there is in the real estate industry and had a fulfilling tenure in sales. Even though I had my sights set on my own brokerage, I did not want to rush the process. I wanted to embrace every season of my career. My rationale was that in the next chapter, I'd have so much to pour into those I impact.

I told myself after ten years in sales, I'd look into opening my own firm. I guess the universe didn't agree with that timeline, because the housing market crashed. So, I grew my skills for two more years with aspirations of *finally* owning my own firm after twelve years in sales. In the Bible, the number twelve is referenced over a hundred times. It's considered the number synonymous with perfection, symbolizing God's power and authority. To me, it's no coincidence that it took twelve years to further realize my dreams. So, though I had other plans slightly earlier, holding on to His unchanging hand, and being patient has genuinely paid off. I opened ICON Realty Group in February of 2016 and it's grown ever since.

Living, Laughing, Loving, and Lesson Learning

As an entrepreneur, you will work harder and longer... learn that reality early. Though *you* determine your schedule, you also determine your success. So expect to get the early worm in the morning and burn the midnight oil late at night. While burning both ends of the candle, you learn valuable lessons that you are able to pass on to your team and family. One lesson we all are probably learning right now is money management. The economy is like an ocean, and when the waves get high, you need to have some sort of savings to stay afloat. It's always exciting to see more numbers *enter* the account than *exit*. When this happens to you, stay humble and do not overspend. My first year of earning six figures as an independent contractor was exciting, but also (financially) scary. I had to learn how to budget and manage money. I had a husband and three small girls. Above all, bills needed to be paid and mouths had to be fed. My husband and I were *both* supposed to be handling the financial responsibilities, but as I learned, he was not holding up his part of the bargain.

By this time, I had become the breadwinner in the family. The increase in funds coming in didn't matter if financial woes still met my doorstep. I'm talking about lights and water being cut off, foreclosure notices, the car potentially being repossessed - those things were the loudest alarms that changes needed to be made. I learned how to budget, but more importantly, I learned how to manage funds. The market is ever-changing. I had to be prepared to thrive in a booming market, but also be equipped when things were stagnant. Most importantly, I always wanted to be able to provide for my girls. Whether they knew it or not, they hustled through the good and bad with us.

The same year I received those notices of cancellations and repossessions, we still had to provide Christmas for our children. That was non-negotiable. We couldn't afford to go to Toys 'R' Us, but we could afford a few small gifts from local stores. I still remember how appreciative they were of those tokens of love.

It's easy to look back on those days and ask how I pressed through, but honestly, I had no time for fear or reservation. I had three little ones looking to me for guidance, lunch money, advice, a ride to practice, and homework help. There was no time to entertain negative thoughts. I didn't say they didn't make their way in though. Let's scroll back a few years.

As mentioned, I married and had children young. During my third pregnancy, I learned my husband was also expecting a child with another woman. His son and our daughter would be born the same year. With learning this news, my world crashed. *'How?'* *'When?'* *'Where?'* were the questions that raced through my mind. I was so consumed with making sure our household was together, I didn't even *think* he had time to be in other places. But ladies, we've all done it: I blamed myself.

I experienced a deep depression. I lost weight, patches of my hair fell out, and I questioned *everything* about myself. *Was I not attractive anymore? Was I pregnant too much? Was I not sexual enough?* I soon realized it wasn't *me* with a problem, but *him*. We married young, but he still had some growing to do. Unfortunately, one of his unwise decisions heavily impacted me. However, when the unexpected happens, that's when your true character shows.

His son, though born from another womb, is my son. I wanted my daughters to know their brother. I wanted him to know he had a home in my home. Other people encouraged me to do otherwise, but this comes back to my faith-based upbringing. That child did not determine how he got here. But since he's been here, he's felt nothing but unconditional and unapologetic love from me.

During that unimaginable, depressive time, I was not myself. I had to lean on my fathers, both spiritual and biological, to press through. My dad reminded me that God is with me. He hasn't forgotten nor forsaken me. It was during these times that I was reminded that, though I was a grown woman, I was still my daddy's little girl. I still needed my father for guidance and advice. With his encouragement, I prayed to God for strength, healing, and the ability to forgive my husband. Through God's deliverance, there was another unexpected birth, me. I was forged into the Catina I am today: strong, confident and determined. I asked Him to allow me to be able to take care of myself and my girls without depending on anyone, unless by choice. Let's just say the Lord answers prayers.

I understand some people may find inspiration outside of religion. Some people do not have a support system to pour into them. There are other sources to find edification: yoga, speaking to a therapist or a trusted friend or relative, physical activity, gardening. Do what makes you happy and what helps you heal. These experiences that brought you down do not define you or conclude your story. They show your strength, especially when you make it to the other side of them.

After 21 years of marriage, I divorced my first husband. I forgave him for the affair and the child, but he hadn't forgiven himself. He struggled with the reality that he fathered a son and became financially strapped with child support. He never completely recovered nor returned to the confident man I fell in love with. This was the beginning of his financial decline and ironically, my incline. And, although this was the greatest hurt and disappointment of my life, it wasn't the reason our marriage failed.

The spirit of adultery never left our home and you should know that spirits travel. Eventually, I found validation and temporary happiness in other places as well. I had become disenchanted with him as a husband, but I respected that he was a loving father to our daughters. This is the main reason the marriage lasted an additional 18 years. He loved his kids and was very present for the hugs, kisses, laughs, meals, PTA meetings, cheerleading and gymnastics practices - many of which I missed due to building a new business. Ultimately, the lack of financial responsibility from my husband, broken vows from us both, and my rapid personal growth brought the marriage to its end.

I remarried in 2015. That relationship did not last long. After six months, I had to go. With this man, I wanted something totally different from my first husband. He was successful, tall, dark, handsome, and well-dressed just like my dad. He wooed me with flowers, gifts, and we took lavish vacations I had only dreamed of. What I thought were characteristics of strength and stability were those of gas lighting, intimidation and aggression. He was abusive. There were signs from day one, but I was in denial because the abuse was never physical. Plus, I was an independent, successful woman that knew her worth. I'd never allow myself to be abused, right? Don't believe the stereotypes and profiles that say that it's the weaker, dependent woman that finds herself with an abusive man. With just the right amount of manipulation, it can happen to anyone. He would instantly change from a kind-hearted and loving gentleman to an unprovoked enraged monster. Ransacking my home, punching holes in the walls, holding me hostage, chasing down my car and coming within inches of crashing into my driver side door, and threatening to hurt anyone I called for help. We sought counseling. He showed up for every session and was seemingly accountable for his actions. He gave many tearful apologies and promises that it would never happen again. I believed him and wanted to see the best in him, but the next episode was always just around the corner. I called for police intervention and protection but never filed charges. I knew his political standing in the community would cause a fire storm of media attention for my girls and me (just as it had for his previous wife) and possibly negatively impact the new brokerage I had just opened. I just wanted out.

The final straw was when he lashed out in front of my oldest daughter. She was afraid. I was afraid. I also knew I could not let my daughters continue to see me tolerate this behavior and think that this is how a marriage should look. Abuse and intimidation are not things a spouse should tolerate. By this time my father had passed away, so I could not go home for advice. However, I knew if he were here, that marriage would have never happened. If you have found yourself in an abusive relationship, get out! He is not going to change. Maya Angelou said it best, "when a person shows you who they are, believe them *the first time.*"

Just when you may feel like you're conquering the world, the world reminds you that you are *in* it, not *on top of* it. I was diagnosed with breast cancer just four months after opening ICON Realty Group. My battle with breast cancer is deeply personal. Generations of women in my family suffered from this disease, including my grandmother, mother, and late older sister. Losing her to breast cancer prompted me to be on top of my health. She passed away at the gracious age of 35, leaving behind seven precious children. She didn't have the resources and understanding to know how severe this disease can be if untreated. After her death, I began getting mammograms and MRIs on a bi-annual basis. The medical recommendation is annual. In December of 2015, I received an MRI that detected no traces of cancer. During a mammogram six months later, I was diagnosed with stage 1 breast cancer. Yeah, it can all change very quickly. And to think - I almost rescheduled that appointment.

That day when I received my diagnosis, I told my doctor to remove both of my breasts. I did not want to risk it. Since the cancer was detected early, I did not have to undergo any chemotherapy or radiation. Ladies, if your family has a history of certain diseases or illnesses, learn about them, and make screening for them a *priority*. It saved my life. Also, I love and miss you, Erica. The kids are doing alright.

After beating breast cancer and my second divorce, I just wanted to focus on Catina. I wasn't dating. I wasn't looking for a man. I just wanted to enjoy bachelorette life and focus on my business. But you know what they say, when the man plans, God laughs. I met my forever, my third husband, at a political fundraiser. It was April 12, 2017. A Tuesday. I was hosting a fundraiser for our state senator sponsored by several of Richmond's top black business owners. I felt a tap on my shoulder from my unbeknown future husband. We conversed at the event, strictly for networking purposes, and exchanged business cards before the night ended. Robert (platonically) offered to get drinks one day soon, so I held him to it. By Friday, I followed up with everyone I connected with at the event, including him. I mentioned getting drinks that night, but he had to take a rain check. He said he was in Ireland. What is a Black man doing in Ireland? Well, when you're a serious golfer like he is, you take flights to the countries where golf is *very* popular and serious players play.

We got to know each other better over the course of many hours-long conversations. We shared the same interests, laughed at the same jokes, and even knew some of the same people since we both grew up in Henrico County. After two failed marriages, it's only obvious my apprehension to give a third one a try. In fact, as we were learning about each other, he was separating from his spouse as well. We both tried to convince the other that we were not trying to get serious or to remarry. I tried to find any reason not to give him a chance.

His reputation could not be challenged. I tried to find someone who spoke negatively of him. Not a soul. He's been a successful entrepreneur since attending Virginia State University and he's a Marine. My father would've loved him.

Because of previous experiences, I even had his credit pulled. His credit was (and still is) better than mine! The representative even told me to keep him. He was the only man since my dad to hold my hand and say, "let's pray". I had no choice but to let my walls down and allow love to win. Did I mention he was also in real estate? With our partnership, our professional pursuits evolved. On June 2, 2018, my work hubby became my real hubby. My firm of ten grew to OUR firm of 62 agents, and in 2021 we launched our Florida division, Luxe Lane. I often say, "I've been married before, but Robert is my first husband."

In addition to working alongside my husband, what has also been beautiful about entrepreneurship for me has been watching growth happen before my eyes. This went from a vision to a boutique firm to a powerhouse in the City of Richmond. I work alongside my husband and above the ambitious eye of my middle daughter, Asha. Having her on the team is the epitome of legacy. It's what any parent wants: to leave an impact on her child, let alone the inspiration to be a business owner. Even though she is my child, she still had to earn her place on the team.

People would assume that Asha would rise to the top easily because she is my daughter; but for that reason, she also had obstacles to overcome. Even when mom is right, the kids learn on their own. In her first year, Asha did not land any sales because she wanted to take a more *modern* approach to real estate sales, which didn't work in her favor. After that experience, she became coachable and ready to learn under me and other veterans in the industry. She earned her respect just like other agents by working hard, self-improving, and persevering. As a mother, and a boss, it is golden to see her thrive as a top-producing agent.

To Asha, never be ashamed of the legacy or the opportunities it has created for you. Your grandfather would say to hold a good name in everything you do, stay humble, and never to compromise your integrity. I'm so proud that you are making me, him, and your family proud. I love you and your sisters with all my heart and being.

Being an entrepreneur in a family, it's also pertinent to understand boundaries. Family members may think because you are in business for yourself that your schedule is flexible and your PTO days are endless. That's not always the reality. When there's a role to be filled, you're filling it. If someone calls out, that could mean you are taking on that person's responsibilities. One thing about being a leader is that you are not above the team; you are one of them. Leaders just don't land at the top; they work their way up there. For this very reason, in case someone drops the ball, you can pick it up and throw it with ease. With that in mind, being a leader is humbling. It also means that I can also help people find work. In the same breath, I have the tough decision of having to let members go when they become a hindrance to the team.

Life is but a dream - and a journey

In the present, we may ask why we are in certain situations, at certain jobs, or with certain people. Eventually, it all makes sense and adds to your story. Had one piece of my story been altered, I'm not sure if it would look like what it is today. I am appreciative of every twist, turn, and detour because it taught me something. Those lessons are now what I carry on to my team, my family, and others who trust me to mentor them. It's not just the lessons that are impactful - but also the people we run across on our day-to-day walk. Have you ever met someone and wondered why they were placed into your life? They could've been a guardian angel, a forewarning to a particular future instance, or just that pick-me-up you needed to push through the day.

As I opened the doors of ICON in 2016, someone told me the encouraging words all entrepreneurs should keep in their hearts. They said, "Not only will God give you the vision. He will give you those who need the vision and those who support the vision." Those few words were just a preview of the success and happiness that I would soon find as a business owner.

Dearest reader, I leave you with this: Life is a trip, so buckle up. Have faith or an outlet to recharge your ambitious batteries. What (and who) is meant for you will find its way to you. As a business owner, you are *of* the team, not *above* it. So don't hang up the boots just yet. You never know when you'll have to put them on when things get muddy. The rewards are always worth the work. And most importantly, don't lose sight of the vision. It won't happen overnight, but when you get to the pinnacle of your career, all those experiences will feel like they happened so fast.

Be authentic. As women we tend to present ourselves as pretty and polished. We do all things with class, grace, style, and decency which can give the misconception that success came quickly and easily to us. The truth is, things get messy behind the scenes. There are challenges, obstacles and sometimes even trauma. My story is one of perseverance, failing forward, learning to dance in puddles, trusting in God and rising no matter what.

Catina pictured with her husband and business partner, Robert Jones
Photo Credit: Phil Andrews

ICON Realty Leadership Team
Photo Credit: Phil Andrews

ICON Realty Leadership Team
Photo Credit: Phil Andrews

MEET CATINA JONES

Catina Jones is the founder and principal broker of ICON Realty Group. With more than 18 years of providing a superior service experience for her clients, Catina and her team are committed to being your advocate and advisor throughout your real estate transaction. Catina's real estate resume includes new construction, urban revitalization, historic and luxury home sales and marketing. As a Richmond native, Catina has insider knowledge of the most coveted neighborhoods and amenities in the area. In March of 2022, Catina was awarded the Master Entrepreneur of the Year award from the Metropolitan Business League. Additionally, she was featured in the May edition of Real Producers Magazine which highlights real estate industry leaders.

Catina Jones

Catina has been the exclusive Listing Agent for multiple builders, developers, non-profit housing organizations and government entities including Richmond Redevelopment & Housing Authority, The City of Petersburg, Virginia Housing Development Authority, Better Housing Coalition, Southside Community Development & Housing Corporation, Health-E Communities LLC and Premiere Homes, just to name a few. Her track record of success has made her an industry leader. Catina serves as a board member for the Home Building Association of Richmond and was appointed to the Virginia Real Estate Board by Governor Ralph Northam in 2020.

Catina launched her real estate career in 2004. Leveraging her sales, marketing, and relationship-building skills, Catina quickly established a high-volume business and was a Top Producer and Distinguished Achiever within her first year in the industry. In 2013, Catina established ICON Realty as a real estate team located in the Fan area of Richmond, VA. In 2016, after tremendous growth and success, ICON opened as a boutique real estate firm in historic Church Hill. Now, ICON is a storefront office in Rocketts Landing with more than 60 licensed REALTORS. ICON provides a vast array of real estate services including residential, luxury, investor portfolio, and commercial sales and marketing.

As a consecutive year Distinguished Achiever and Top Producer, she maintains an exceptional reputation and track record of success founded on integrity, hard work, commitment, experience, and results. Catina's clients view her as their complete real estate resource and count on her to help them expertly navigate the buying and selling process. It is with great pride and pleasure that she is "Serving the City on the James".

Keep in touch with Catina:

Facebook: Catina Jones
Instagram: @catinajones_ceo
LinkedIn: Catina (Hawkins) Jones
Website: iconrealtyrva.com

Acknowledgements

Amari Wright
The Wright Notary, LLC
Website: www.amarithenotary.com

Ashanti Wright

Arlette Hawkins
Website: Arletting.Wordpress.com
Facebook: Arlette Hawkins
Instagram: @only_arlette
LinkedIn: Arlette Hawkins

Kimberly R. Baine
LinkedIn: Kimberly Baine

Laneé Prentice
Facebook: Laneé Johnson Prentice
Instagram: @Laneejprentice
LinkedIn: Laneé Prentice

Michelle Johnson

Robert Jones
ICON Commercial
Website: www.iconcommercialrva.com
Facebook: Robert D Jones II
Instagram: @RobertDJonesii

Kim Martin
KLM SCHOLARSHIP FOUNDATION
Website: www.KLMfoundation.org
Facebook: @klmscholarshipfoundation
Instagram: @klmsf
LinkedIn: KLM Scholarship Foundation

Dakia Knight
The KEY Team @ ICON Realty Group
Website: www.thekeysinrichmond.com
Facebook: @TheKeysinRichmond
Instagram: @kiagotkeys
LinkedIn: Dakia Knight

Born into my Greatness
Holly Byrd Miller

In a rural area within Tappahannock, Virginia, I was born to Carl and Viola (aka Connie). Unwed and young, 16 and 18 respectively, they loved each other immensely and were committed to raising my biological sister (Anetra) and me, despite a lack of resources, education or money. Eventually, they adopted two other children from within our family and I gained another sister (Arlice) and a brother (Philip). Dad and mom gave us a loving household and a foundation that would later shape who I would become as an entrepreneur.

At the age of 16, dad dropped out of high school to take care of his family. We were poor and lived in a four-room house with no fully functioning toilet. Dad made ends meet the best way he knew how by working entry-level construction jobs. After years of working in construction, gaining valuable experience, and having the drive and determination to create a better life for his family, my dad formed his own construction company. The years that followed were my introductions into entrepreneurism.

Dad owned CD Byrd, Inc. He had employees and was a small business subcontractor working in the state of Virginia. I remember the times when he started to become more successful in his business. He started to acquire more opportunities and, hence, more wealth. Although dad was starting to successfully grow his business, I did not have aspirations to be an entrepreneur at that time. I did not want to work seven days a week with few vacations or time off. Dad had a very strong work ethic. I saw his business failures, like overstaffing, undercharging for his services and most importantly, not properly tracking his financial records. However, I also saw him expand his service offerings. Despite having a limited high school education, he had the foresight to grow a multi-million dollar business. **He understood his market and he understood the problems and needs of his target audience. Dad also provided services that complemented his core services, which eliminated the need to outsource, all of which increased his net revenue.** He taught me how to grow a business from the ground up and build a family legacy. I started to see the fruits of his labor in the lifestyle we were living.

Activity: When you think about starting or growing a business, jot down one to two focus areas. By each of those products or services, identify your strengths and weaknesses. Now jot down how you think you can change the weaknesses into strengths. If you don't know how to identify those strengths and weaknesses, keep reading.

Finding your Passion

From a young age, I struggled with being overweight which caused me to have insecurities. Growing up, my nickname was *Porky*. I did not like it, but because I was called it most of my childhood and teenage years, I learned to accept it and it became part of my identity. At the age of 12, my mom allowed me to dabble in her makeup. I loved makeup because it didn't matter what my weight was, makeup was the great equalizer. It didn't matter what the scale said, makeup made me feel pretty from the inside-out.

At the age of 16, my makeup skills started to catch the attention of friends and family. I conducted my first wedding makeup for my cousin Jackie who married Maurice. I fell in love with the idea of someone entrusting me to help her look her best on such a special occasion. I did Jackie's makeup and she felt and looked pretty. That was the beginning of discovering my passion for helping others look and feel their best.

As I started to build my makeup clientele, I became more and more inspired, encouraged and excited by the fact that I was helping people look and *feel* beautiful. I was taught to see the beauty in everyone and now I was helping them see the beauty in themselves. More and more clients would say to me, **"you really love your job and it shows because you are beaming." After hearing that repeatedly, I knew that beauty and personal branding was not only my passion but also my purpose.**

Activity: List one to two things that bring you immense joy. It's a great way to determine your passion. Starting a business by leading with passion is a great way to attain success.

Education

After I graduated high school, I had no plans. I had become complacent living in my small hometown and worked as a cashier at the local KFC. Fast forward two years, my sister (Anetra) graduated high school and decided she wanted to go to Braxton Business School. I decided she wasn't going to outdo me. Imposter syndrome set in, so I decided I needed to start business school too. I enrolled in ECPI Computer School.

I attended ECPI for nine months and received a medical computer specialist certification. I was able to immediately secure my first professional job working for a medical transcription company. I worked my way up from an entry level position, as a medical transcriptionist, to the office manager. I worked there for eight years.

Young Adult Life

I was dating a micro celebrity in the Washington, DC area and the insecurities about my weight (that I had suppressed) started to surface again. I spent a lot of time surrounded by models, actors and singers. One day, I looked in the mirror and started crying. I felt like the fattest, most hideous person on the planet. I hated the way I looked in the mirror. I saw the amount of cellulite I allowed to take over my body. I couldn't stop obsessing over the stretch marks and my overextended belly and thighs that were rubbing together. I really detested the person I saw in the mirror. It was at that moment I decided to lose weight. I wanted to look like the models that surrounded me. Within 30 days, I lost 30 pounds and went down six dress sizes. I was barely eating 500 calories a day and working out two times a day. I would never recommend anyone take such drastic measures. It was a real low for me. However, I got down to a size 6, which made me feel a lot better about what I saw in the mirror. That really helped with my physical self-esteem.

Activity: Is there something you don't like about yourself? Something that takes a toll on your self-esteem? If yes, jot it down or say it out loud. Now, make a conscious decision to change it. You are in charge of your own happiness. Don't take as drastic measures as me with my rapid, unhealthy weight loss, but simply take action and own your greatness. If you don't, you will continue to speak negatively to/about yourself and you will allow others to do the same. Live your best life by living the best for yourself first and then choose with whom you will allow to join your journey towards a positive self-esteem and self-worth.

In December of 1999, I relocated to Northern Virginia. My circle of peers and professionals started to broaden. Again, imposter syndrome was rearing its ugly head. I was taking on the aspirations of the people who surrounded me in the DMV. I met other 20 somethings who were highly ambitious, had attended college, and worked high powered jobs. Surrounding yourself with like-minded people who are ambitious and want to make positive impacts in life is something I highly recommend you do. However, if you suffer from imposter syndrome and haven't dealt with your insecurities, they will surface. I was becoming more and more insecure about my lack of higher education. Although I had a lucrative job working as a healthcare regional manager, and I had my own car and apartment, I was still insecure about not having a college degree. I avoided questions about college. These were some of the best and worst years of my life. I worked really hard to fit in with this highly competitive professional environment, but I never allowed myself to feel like I belonged.

One of the most successful people I spent time with was an NBA basketball player. We developed a strong friendship. One day he referred to me as a people pleaser and concluded that I suffered from imposter syndrome. Initially, I was devastated by his comment, but it later turned out to be the best thing he could have ever said to me. It gave me the push I needed to start doing the work to figure out my own happiness. Self-acceptance and discovering self-worth are things we all owe ourselves.

Activity: List a time in your life when you were a people pleaser and/or suffered from imposter syndrome. What did that experience look like? How did you overcome it? If you haven't overcome it, make a conscious effort to identify it and do something to change it.

Life is a personal marathon and you are the only runner. Be kind to yourself by giving yourself grace to run your race.

The Love of My Life

I met Floyd on Friday, August 29th, 2003. Who knew a request for my parking spot would lead to meeting the man who would change my life forever? After dating long distance for six months, we got engaged. We were married on August 30, 2005.

Floyd is the President and CEO of the Metropolitan Business League which is a non-profit, membership-based business association that creates business connections in Central Virginia. They foster business development and expansion for small, women and minority-owned businesses. Floyd has always been my biggest supporter and always wants me to be the best version of myself. He too quickly realized I had one final insecurity that was still holding me back: not having my college degree. He encouraged me to attend Averett University full-time while working full-time for the United Network for Organ Sharing.

With his support, I graduated with a business degree with honors, Summa Cum Laude. I will always remember being handed my diploma by one of my favorite college administrators, Nancy Atkins. She was a great mentor and I remain grateful for her mentorship.

Activity: List one to three mentors who have helped to shape the person you have become. If you don't have a mentor, I highly recommend you seek one who you trust will help you navigate life and/or business. The proper guidance can prove to be invaluable to your success.

Think Like an Entrepreneur

I continued to work full-time at the United Network for Organ Sharing. With a business degree, I learned entrepreneurial strategies. Thanks to the influence of my dad, coupled with my newly acquired business degree, I started to think more like an entrepreneur.

With the promise of building teams and attaining success, I started dabbling in multilevel marketing. I learned a lot about developing a business acumen, but I also realized I would never work my way to the top as a top earner. I was still committed to my love of beauty and I wanted to create my own blueprint and my legacy. In February 2012, I established Makeup by Holly, LLC. I started offering makeup services for weddings and special occasions. I also partnered with local photographers who offered personal branding services. Personal branding was becoming more popular because clients wanted to have a competitive visual appeal to help them attract their target audience.

Personal Branding Tips:
- Know your target audience's pain points
- Utilize keywords, images and videos to provide solutions to their problems
- Invest in professional image consulting services, high-resolution images and video to establish yourself as a professional
- Establish yourself as a subject matter expert by offering education, resources and highlighting how you helped other clients grow

As I was traveling around the country, working for my corporate job, I was also building my beauty and personal branding business. Oftentimes, I would travel to a location and stay over an extra day or go in slightly earlier to take a training class or meet with a branding prospect. This really allowed me to start building the foundation and blueprint for how I would grow my business nationally. Of course, I was doing this legally and on my own dime, but I was at least able to minimize the travel cost because I was already traveling to these locations for corporate business.

As I was quickly growing Makeup by Holly, I realized I needed to immerse myself in the beauty industry, so I started freelancing for Saks Fifth Avenue as a freelance makeup artist. I became a certified makeup instructor for LB Beauty Academy in Richmond, Virginia, where I was training the next generation of makeup artists.

To ensure I stayed on my A-game, I invested in intensive, hands-on workshops with Derrick Rutledge (the current makeup artist to Oprah). I also studied under Oprah's previous makeup artist (Reggie Wells) with whom I still have a special friendship/mentorship. I also spent time learning from Sir John (makeup artist to Beyoncé'). I studied at the Make Up Forever Academy and continue to take refresher classes at the International Beauty Show and the Makeup Show. I was well on my way to becoming a nationally recognized personal branding and image consulting expert.

Beauty Tips:
- Establish a skincare regimen that compliments your skin type
- Exfoliate at least once per week to reveal your best skin
- Choose makeup colors that compliment your skin tone and undertone
- Wash your makeup brushes at least once per week
- Throw away makeup and skincare that has surpassed the printed expiration date
- Dress to compliment your body type

- Choose a hairstyle that frames your face shape

Activity: List experts who are doing work you aspire to do. Contact them to see if you can purchase at least 15 minutes of their time and schedule a consultation. Make sure you have your questions written down in advance so you don't forget to ask them. Also, hire a business coach. Choose wisely by asking for references and metrics that determine success.

To Whom Much is Given, Much is Required

As I continued to apply the makeup techniques and business acumen I learned from Derek, Reggie and Sir John, my company started to attract lots of attention from executives, corporations and professionals throughout the nation. It was becoming harder and harder to decline the abundance of job opportunities: from prepping keynote speakers for conferences and speaking engagements, to providing beauty and branding services to panel members, conference attendees, headshots for corporations, executives, nonprofits and other professionals to providing beauty services for brides. I knew I needed to create a national team and fast. I started to bring in other makeup artists, hair stylists, wardrobe stylists, as well as videographers and photographers. Makeup By Holly became Makeup by Holly Beauty Partners.

Similar to what I learned from dad, I expanded our service offerings. By broadening my workforce, they were helping us to meet the needs of our growing client base. That proved to be a game changer for our business model and started to grow our revenue exponentially, as well as our client portfolio.

I learned it was really important to bring in team members who are like-minded, ambitious, hard-working, and professional. I learned valuable lessons: don't employ staff who don't share your vision or work ethic; surround yourself with staff that fully support the vision and give them ownership for their roles and responsibilities. Networking and employing like-minded professionals proved to be invaluable for a positive culture and overall success of my business.

Activity: List the organizations, churches and/or groups you can network with to grow. Contact them and start conversations about strategic partnerships.

Business Resources: Metropolitan Business League, Chamber of Commerce, Small Business Administration, S.C.O.R.E.

Coming Out of Depression

In May of 2017, I received one of the hardest phone calls I could've received. My dad was in the hospital. Floyd, my sisters, brother, mom and I rushed to the hospital where we would spend the next three days with our family members. It was repeatedly confirmed that dad suffered a severe brain aneurysm and the damage was irreversible. My dad had Type II Diabetes and although he managed it with medication, he never managed it with proper diet and exercise. Devastatingly, the family and I would need to make the decision about the end of life.

Over the next month, I grieved dad's death. I went into a state of depression that I've never experienced before. I lost the first love of my life and the man who taught me how to become the entrepreneur I am today. With love and support from my husband, mom, family and friends, I started to dig my way out of depression because I knew Dad would want me to live a happy life. I poured myself into work. I employed his hard work ethic. I could feel his presence and his guidance continuously with me, all of which helped me build a substantial client portfolio throughout the country and secure the status of international makeup artist and speaker.

Tip: If you want to grow your business internationally, consider the following:

1) Partner with a company that is hosting an international retreat
2) Secure an opportunity to speak, even if it's only 15-30 minutes
3) Secure sponsorship opportunities, either monetarily or by donating time or talent
4) Network with local business owners to establish relationships and learn the business culture while visiting the country

As I threw myself completely into my business, it inevitably continued to grow and it became harder to maintain my corporate job. I was traveling around the country, meeting with roughly 100 clients and generating more than one million dollars annually. In 2018, I had a conversation with my husband, discussing the need to create an exit strategy from my corporate job. I started shifting my mindset from working a corporate job to being a full-time entrepreneur continuously building my business. Being the mentor he is, Floyd knew I needed to have access to quality health insurance and the revenue to support walking away from my corporate job, which was supplying a generous salary, plus benefits, paid time off and all of the luxuries that I had acquired. He needed to make sure my business could support the lifestyle we had become accustomed to. Collectively, we created a strategy to exit corporate. The strategy consisted of establishing business goals and milestones, finalizing a business plan, creating a budget, making maximum contributions into my 401(k), and using paid time off to meet with clients and attend business trainings. We set revenue projections for my business that surpassed my corporate salary year-over-year. My business income and revenue also continuously surpassed my corporate salary as a business development manager.

In January 2020, I reached a pivotal point as I was nearing the time I was going to make the definitive decision about walking away from my corporate job. I was getting cold feet due to job security. However, my annual review from my new Director was poor, despite the fact that I had met my revenue goals. It was becoming increasingly difficult to show up to my corporate job. Building a relationship with my new Director was also difficult and I found myself coming home in tears dealing with the anxiety from my job. I didn't realize it at the time, but God was positioning me to walk away from that job. He knew that if He didn't push me, I likely would have tried to stay there longer than I should.

Little did I know, my Director was positioning me to be fired. That was new to me because I had never been fired from any job. I had always excelled in everything I did professionally. I knew it was time to leave, so I put in my two weeks' notice. As fate would have it, I wasn't required to complete my two weeks. I left within the week and was paid in full for the next two months, with full access to healthcare, while I settled into becoming a full-time entrepreneur. Even though Covid hit in March 2020, leaving in February 2020 to become a full-time entrepreneur was still the best decision I could have made. I was giving myself time to pivot, be strategic and intentional about the growth and overall success of the business. As I write this book, we have increased our business revenue by 257% since leaving my corporate job and pursuing my business full-time.

Activity: List a time when you were feeling defeated or like you were about to be fired or you just felt like your corporate job was no longer the place that you should be spending your time and expertise. What did that feel like when you either overcame that challenge or you walked away and decided that you were going to do something different? If you are feeling that way now and haven't done anything about it, I encourage you to make a concise plan and pursue it.

Mentoring and Networking

I believe in mentoring and networking in order to achieve a successful business and build legacy. I mentor my Beauty Partners and I network with like-minded professionals. We leverage the collective expertise of one another.

Moreover, I network with other companies that offer complimenting services. I believe in community over competition and also believe there is enough opportunity for all of us. **When I decided to leave my corporate job in February 2020**, I was renewed.

I also partnered with MLR. MLR is based in Boston, MA and is owned and operated by Lou Rod Cueva. For 10 years, MLR has created next level experiences through hair, makeup, grooming and photography services around the country for conferences, trade shows and festivals nationwide.

In February 2022, I celebrated 10 years in business and I feel like I'm just getting started. My definition of success is building a business that gives me freedom to prioritize my personal life.

I hope as you are reading this book, something has been written that inspires you to live out your passion and purpose. I hope you feel empowered to authentically be yourself and not suffer from imposter syndrome. Always follow your God-given purpose for an enriched life that allows you to achieve success and build a legacy for your family, community and beyond.

Activity: List one to five people who you would consider champions and cheerleaders in your life and in your business. Then list one to five people for whom you are champions, cheerleaders and mentors in their lives and in their business. Continue to show up for one another!

Holly Byrd Miller pictured with Client Michelle Williams, Former member of Destiny's Child

Holly with husband (Floyd) and their fur baby (Carl).
Photo credit: Raleigh Desper of Raleigh Marketing

Makeup by Holly Beauty Partners
(not all are pictured; as this book went to print, there are 40 across
the nation)
Photo credit: Raleigh Desper, Raleigh Marketing (also pictured)

MEET HOLLY BYRD MILLER

Holly Byrd Miller is the **CEO and Founder of Makeup by Holly, LLC DBA Makeup by Holly B Partners**. She has an award-winning Beauty business and leads a global team of Branding and Beauty professionals who Educate, Consult and Curate signature looks and Brand Strategies for brands, executives and corporations. The team is comprised of licensed hair stylists, certified and professional makeup artists, personal wardrobe stylists, photographers, videographers and Brand Strategists.

Holly Byrd Miller

Holly's professional career started over 25 years ago in Corporate America, managing multi-million dollar portfolios annually for healthcare companies located around the United States. Holly's areas of expertise are Communications, Business Development, Sales and Marketing. She has a proven track record of creating strategies for maximizing time and profits.

Holly started her professional beauty career freelancing for luxury international companies: Giorgio Armani Beauty, Yves Saint Laurent, Chanel and Laura Mercier. Holly was a representative/distributor for direct sales brands: Younique Cosmetics, Rodan & Fields, and Jeunesse Global. She trained with Brand Ambassadors for Yves Saint Laurent, Giorgio Armani Beauty, Chanel, as well as the Makeup For Ever Academy New York, trained one-on-one with Derrick Rutledge (Oprah's current makeup artist), as well as one-on-one with Reggie Wells (former makeup artist to Oprah Winfrey), and completed a Master Class with Sir John (celebrity artist to Beyonce, Chrissy Teigen and Joan Small).

Currently, Holly is also the Chief Operating Officer for MLR Agency located in Boston, MA, an experience and production agency providing activations through hair and makeup for global brands and corporations.

Keep in touch with Holly:

Facebook: Holly Byrd Miller
Instagram: @makeupbyholly
LinkedIn: Makeup by Holly B Partners
Website: www.makeupbyhollyb.com

Acknowledgements

BK Fulton
Soulidifly Productions
www.Soulidifly.com
Facebook: @bkfulton
Instagram: @bkfulton
LinkedIn: bkfulton

Gwen Hurt
Shoe Crazy Wine and Spirits
Website: www.shoecrazywine.com
Facebook: @shoecrazywine
Instagram: @shoecrazywine
LinkedIn: Gwen Hurt

Raleigh Desper
Raleigh Desper LLC
Website: photographywithraleigh.com
Facebook: @Raleighmarketing247
Instagram: @photographywithraleigh
LinkedIn: Raleigh Desper

Jacquie Lopez
Jacquie's Boutique
Website: www.jacquiesboutique.com
Instagram: @jacquie_boutique

Tierra Parker
She is Beautee by Tierra
Facebook: @Tierra Parker Hickman
Instagram: @Sheis_tierradesiree
LinkedIn: Tierra Parker

Sydnii Robinson
Sydnii CharManes

Instagram: @scmanez

Angela Patton
Girls For A Change
Website: girlsforachange.org
Facebook: @girlsforachange
Instagram: @girlsforachange
LinkedIn: Angela Patton

Lisa Rine
Hollywood's Hair Studio
Facebook: Hollywood's Hair Studio
Instagram: @hollywoodshairstudio
LinkedIn: Lisa Rine

Saraellen Bagby
JBella Photograghy
Website: https://jbellaphotography.zenfolio.com/
Facebook: @JBELLARVA
Instagram: @JBELLA_PHOTOGRAPHYRVA
LinkedIn: Saraellen Bagby

Ivory Morgan-Burton
Storybook Events
Website: www.storybookevents.net
Facebook: @storybookeventsnorfolk
Instagram: @ivorymorganburton
LinkedIn: ivorymorganburton

Amy Garelick
POWER UP Video Studios
Website: powerupvideo.com
Facebook: @powerupvideo
Instagram: @powerupvideo
https://www.linkedin.com/in/amygarelick/

KK Shoaf
Whole Life Beauty LLC
Website: wholelifebeauty.biz
Facebook: @WholeLifeBeauty
Instagram: @wholelifebeauty
LinkedIn: KK Shoaf

Sheila Ivey
S. I. Beauty Studio
Website: Siveybeautystudio.com
Facebook: Sheila Ivey
Instagram: @Onetouchabove
LinkedIn: Sheila Ivey

Sydnii Robinson
PrettyVicious Enterprises
Instagram: @prettyviciousglam

Anetra Byrd
Neechic
Website: www.neechicstyles.com
Facebook: @Neechic
Instagram: @Neechic
LinkedIn: Neechic

Angela Jackson
Beauty by Angela J
Facebook: @beautybyangelaj
Instagram: @beautybyangelaj
LinkedIn: Angela Jackson

Stephanie Smith
LB Beauty Academy
Website: Lbbeautyacademy.com
Facebook: @lbbeautyacademy
Instagram: @lbbeauty2

LinkedIn: LB Beauty Academy

DeNita L. Turner
Image Builders, Inc
Website: Denitaturner.com
Facebook: @denitaturner
Instagram: @denita.turner.301

Floyd Miller
Metropolitan Business League
Website: www.thembl.org

A Journey toward Grace
Grace Washington

I was thrilled to be invited to share my story of success among such a powerful group of successful women. I hope my contribution will resonate with everyone but especially the more "mature" audience. I want it to be a testimony that it is never too late to pursue your dreams. You can't go back and start from the beginning, but you can start where you are and change the ending. I am Grace Washington, President and CEO of J&G Workforce Development Services, LLC. We are a national consulting firm that specializes in providing services in Section 3, Workforce Development and Engagement among other services.

The Long Journey Begins

My journey has been long. I have had extreme successes, and sadly, extreme failures. That comes with the territory if you are going to be an entrepreneur. My complete story would take far more space than I am allowed for this contribution. I consider myself a serial entrepreneur, having been a real estate investor, owned an entertainment production company, owned and operated a minority newspaper, owned a chain of 30 minute tune up shops, a mental health company and now a national consulting firm. In addition, I had a successful corporate career. I believe I have forgotten more than most people will ever experience. I have been blessed beyond measure.

What is success? For me, success includes not only your professional life or how much money you are making but also your personal life, as the success in your personal life many times is what will sustain you through the trials and tribulations of owning your own business. My road to success started early with strong support and a sense of self instilled by my mother, Margaret Brown. From a young age my mother used to tell me that there was no such word as can't. She always encouraged my siblings and I to speak correct English and would correct us when we said the word "ain't". So, when she would tell me there was no such word as can't, I thought it truly was not a word. Can you imagine how powerful that was in my early life? If the word did not exist, **there was nothing that I could *NOT* do, as the word did not exist**. A single parent of five girls, my mother also instilled the value of having a strong work ethic. She would often work two jobs, and once even a third job, to make sure her family was provided for. She was a Chef - not a cook, but an esteemed, respectable Chef - in the early days when Black women were not filling those roles. She started my older sister and me working when we were both 12 years old. Most of all, my mother filled our home with love and taught each of us that love for ourselves and others was indeed the most important thing. Through the years my mother and my sisters have supported me in every adventure I have ever embarked. They often worked alongside me in the businesses. If I was doing it, my entire family was involved at some level, even during the times when my businesses did not work out or I was having a tough time. It was/is so gratifying to wake up every day and know that I had the support of five to seven people in my life no matter what.

Guidance and Motivation = MENTOR

Another instrumental contribution to my success has been the presence of strong mentors in my life. I met my first husband, Al Mack Washington when I was 18 years old. He was and is still to this day the most intelligent and capable person I have ever met in my life. Earlier, when I mentioned I was a serial entrepreneur, most of those businesses were with him. He was creative, hard driving and the best salesperson ever. We had such fun starting and running new businesses through the years. Unfortunately, I lost him to brain cancer after 23 years of marriage. I was devastated having lost the love of my life. He had taught me everything I knew about business and life up to that point; he was my first mentor. **Having a mentor to guide you is paramount to success in business.** A mentor could be a personal or professional coach or an organization that specializes in mentoring small and emerging businesses. I also found books to be an excellent tool. A couple of my favorites are *The Secret* by Rhonda Byrne and *The 7 Habits of Highly Effective People* by Stephen Covey.

My latest adventure into entrepreneurship started in 2006 when I left my very successful high paying corporate job. I took my life savings and invested it all in real estate in Petersburg, Virginia. The market was red hot! I believed I had the formula and was on my way to making millions! Properties were cheap in Petersburg. Everyone was buying and renovating them. I had remarried and my husband owned a construction company. How could we fail? I was humming along until I realized that there were people living in the run down properties we were purchasing. I was instantly convinced! It was almost like a spiritual conversion. I knew from that moment on that I had to do something to try to impact and change the lives of those living in such poverty. **If you are fortunate enough to mix passion and purpose in your business, it is another key to success.** I now had mine. The first thing I did was create a construction trades training program to train and hire the residents on our renovation projects as I found that many of the residents had multiple barriers that blocked them from employment. Doing something to assist in removing or working around those barriers became my overwhelming mission.

In Hard Times, There is Always a Guiding Light

Well, soon there were rumors of a recession. By 2008 I had purchased a total of 40 properties and they were in varying stages of renovation. In early 2009 the market crashed. We were not prepared and I didn't know what to do. I tried to hang on for as long as I could. Then in December of 2009, my mother died unexpectedly! There are no words to express how devastated I was and still am. I was in a fog - having lost all my money, my precious mother, my strongest supporter, and ultimately I realized I was in a bad marriage. It was all so surreal making funeral arrangements for my mother while the bank was calling me on the other line threatening foreclosure! The constant that kept me going was the love of my family. By this time, I had two beautiful grandbabies. I had been fortunate to see them both come into the world. I didn't have any money, but I was successful in a part of my personal life. However, I continued to pursue my passion. When I couldn't help myself, I was still working to help others. The Construction Trades training program that I had created helped to support us for the next several years as I was able to get multiple contracts throughout the region. The pursuit of assisting to provide economic pathways for our underserved communities was an all-consuming passion. This passion led me to get more involved in workforce development, as training without a job didn't mean anything and I was in search of the answer. I researched every workforce development entity and I discovered they were not serving the residents I wanted to serve, so what were they doing? If no one was serving them, how could they ever pull themselves up by their bootstraps? The reality was: they didn't even have any boots!

So What the Heck is Section 3?

One day while searching the internet, I stumbled on HUD Section 3. What is Section 3? Section 3 is the legal basis for providing jobs for residents and awarding contracts to businesses in areas receiving certain types of HUD financial assistance. It fosters local economic development, neighborhood economic improvement, and individual self-sufficiency. In layman's terms, it means that if federal dollars are being spent, they are supposed to hire low-income workers and small, low-income businesses to work on those projects. It literally was the answer I was looking for. I became a Section 3 consultant that day! Now I had an official name for what I wanted to do, as it was more than training and it was more than workforce development! Guess what? There were no organized Section 3 consultants in the Richmond, Virginia area and very few even across the country. However, none of them were delivering the services like I had planned. I had found my niche! I printed some brochures and business cards that very day and now all I needed to do was find clients to pay me for my services. Hard Work, Perseverance, and Passion had gotten me to this point. My next steps would be crucial.

Networking and building authentic relationships with other like-minded business professionals is also another critical aspect of building and sustaining a successful business. Along my entrepreneurial journey, I had met Mike Hopkins of the M Companies/Emerge Construction in the pursuit of some other opportunities. He was putting together the RFP response for the Black History Museum and Cultural Center. Together we worked for months to develop a plan to secure the contract. He was ultimately awarded the project and we were able to deliver the most successful Section 3 project ever in the City of Richmond. Alas, I had secured a paid contract! Most importantly, that experience allowed me to really figure out the gaps that existed in the delivery of Section 3 services. I

97

received tremendous back lash and attacks from those who had worked to facilitate Section 3 previously. I remember one person telling me that it was not work that a woman should do - imagine that! However, my passion and purpose to find a way to assist those who needed help allowed me to push on undeterred.

Time to Level Up

I knew my passion and I knew our delivery of services were worth paying for. Now all I had to do was secure more contracts. Timing was good as Richmond had several affordable housing or HUD projects in the pipeline. We were able to secure contracts with the City of Richmond and with three of the affordable housing developments. So now I had a little room to work on improving and upgrading our delivery of services. Section 3 is about compliance so as a consulting firm most other firms only repeated what the goals were. We documented what and where the gaps existed and proceeded to develop solutions to those gaps. One such discovery was that there was no entity that was keeping demographic information on the residents or businesses that met Section 3 requirements. It came back to the authentic relationships that you build along the way as an entrepreneur. One such relationship was with Carol Reese of ReeSource, Inc. Together we developed a tool that allowed us to better serve our clients. The partnership and creation of that tool won us the League Leadership Award from the Metropolitan Business League in 2018. Identifying and working with community stakeholders and partners has also been a key component in our success. Our work with Floyd Miller and the Metropolitan Business League, Pat Foster, City of Richmond, Minority Business, and now Caprichia Moses, Office of Community Wealth has been especially monumental in propelling our company forward. Moreover, I certainly cannot forget our partners at Richmond Redevelopment and Housing Authority (RRHA). I appreciate the trust they have in J&G to allow us access to their communities to help the residents. These are examples of great partnerships which are crucial to the growth and sustainment of any business.

Stay Positive!

In 2018 we were invited to participate in the engagements portion of the Navy Hill development project. The project proposed to create thousands of jobs for the very communities I was serving. I was all in, committed 100%, to assisting with making this happen. We spent the next two years involved in the most negative political battle ever. We eventually lost the battle. However, I was able to grow our company from the income we earned. I must give a huge shout out to Michelle Mosby of Help Me Help You (HMHY) for bringing J&G to the table and being such a fantastic negotiator which allowed me to be paid my worth! Again, it's those authentic relationships you develop along the way.

Time to Pivot

In 2020, Covid hit. I took the opportunity to close my mental health company and focus 100% of my energy on J&G and our Section 3 business. We were fortunate to secure a loan through SBA to fund J&G while we grew our business. The first thing we had to do was to figure out how to offer our services virtually in the pandemic. Once we were able to do that, we were then able to offer our service outside of Richmond. In early 2020, I was contacted by an acquaintance who asked me to participate in an RFP response for RRHA. That led to a partnership with The Richman Group that enabled us to expand our business nationwide and even to the US Virgin Islands. Shout out to Glenn Hudson and Andre Blakely. Soon we were receiving requests from other developers across the country as we continued to grow our company. Oh, and remember the Navy Hill project that was so negative. The same developer connected with me and I am working with them on two major projects in Richmond and

Henrico, Virginia. This speaks volumes to what happens when you maintain class and professionalism in spite of negativity. While we are human, so it's not always easy to do, it is imperative for the company's reputation.

We have continued to expand the services we offer and to improve on our delivery of those services. We now offer Section 3, Davis Bacon, Workforce Development, Relocation, Strategic Planning, and Engagement/Outreach services. In 2022 we have been invited to participate in RFP responses on three different projects each over two billion dollars. In 2021 and 2022 I was invited to speak at the National Association of Housing and Redevelopment (NAHRO), Public Housing Authorities Directors Association (PHADA), and conferences on the subject of Section 3 cementing us as subject matter experts in this field.

Beautiful Endings and Exciting Beginnings

As President and CEO of J&G Workforce Development Services, I am proud to say that today we are better than ever and all because I was led to help others! I have always been passionate about service to others and making money. What kept me going through the hard times was a vision and a purpose bigger than me. With the unwavering support of my family, I am a successful single woman. I have four beautiful sisters, who - if you know me - you probably have met along the way. We're most often referred to as "The Sisters" - Jennifer, Lisa, Charlotte, and Tina. I'm grateful for my precious daughter and son-in-love, Gracie and Mike Bogar, and my four grandchildren, Allee, Grace (yes, another Grace), Gabby, Aiden and Gianna. I would be remiss if I didn't mention the hard work and commitment of my internal team: Jennifer Johnson, Erica McCray, Travis Booker, Freddie Robertson and Joyce Paige. My external team, Carol Reese, Joli Aslan and Wes Dewalt, are equally important. I cannot fit in all that has transpired through the years or the wonderful people encountered along the way. So I'll end with this: Steve Jobs said as some of his final words, "Treasure love for your family, love for your spouse, love for your friends. Treat yourself well and cherish others." And as the good book states, "the greatest of these is LOVE." 1 Corinthians 13:13

Grace Washington

Grace pictured with Floyd Miller of Metropolitan Business League

Grace pictured with her family

MEET GRACE WASHINGTON

Grace Washington has more than 30 years' experience as an executive and business development leader. Grace is the CEO of J&G Workforce Development, which is located in Richmond, VA. Under Grace's leadership, the company has developed a reputation as a leader in HUD Section 3 & Relocation Compliance Consulting, Community Engagement Strategic Planning and Execution, and Workforce Development.

Grace formed J&G Workforce Development, LLC in 2016, answering a call to provide job and skill training in the construction industry to our underserved communities. Grace transitioned into Workforce Development after spending 10 years in Real Estate Development where she recognized that the lack of skilled tradespersons in the construction industry was also an opportunity for unemployed and underemployed individuals in underserved communities.

Through her membership involvement in the Metropolitan Business League (MBL), Grace strengthened its outreach to the construction community. She was instrumental in developing their successful **"Construction Build Up"** Program, which assists contractor members to build capacity enabling them to successfully connect additional contract opportunities. Grace's efforts to extend professional development opportunities to subcontractors were rewarded with the 2018 MBL Leadership Award.

Grace continues to promote and develop economic opportunities for underrepresented groups in construction. Grace remains a passionate advocate for all individuals seeking career and contract opportunities in construction. Additionally, Grace has made a deliberate effort to increase regional awareness related to women in the construction industry. In 2022, Grace planned and co-hosted MBL's first Women in Construction Summit.

Grace is the proud mother of one daughter, Gracetta II. Her daughter and son-in-law, Mike Bogar, have blessed her with four beautiful grandchildren.

Conclusion

Congratulations! You made it to the end of this book which attests to your commitment to starting or growing your business. We hope that you've been inspired by the stories contained within and have gained a sense of motivation to pursue your entrepreneurial dreams. Remember, becoming a business owner is bigger than you. It's a testament to the legacy of what was, what is and what is to come. Your clients, customers, community and family are waiting on you to impact the world with your gift and create a legacy for generations to come. Are you going to let them down?

Made in the USA
Middletown, DE
11 October 2022